2012 CODING WORKBOOK

for the Physician's Office

Alice Covell, CMA-A (AAMA), RMA, CPC

Australia • Brazil • Japan • Korea • Mexico • Singapore • Spain • United Kingdom • United States

2012 Coding Workbook for the Physician's Office
Alice Covell

Vice President, Careers & Computing: Dave Garza
Director of Learning Solutions: Matthew Kane
Acquisitions Editor: Rhonda Dearborn
Managing Editor: Marah Bellegarde
Product Manager: Amy Wetsel
Editorial Assistant: Lauren Whalen
Vice President, Marketing: Jennifer Baker
Marketing Director: Wendy Mapstone
Senior Marketing Manager: Nancy Bradshaw
Marketing Coordinator: Piper Huntington
Production Manager: Andrew Crouth
Design and Content Project Management: PreMediaGlobal

© 2013 Delmar, Cengage Learning

ALL RIGHTS RESERVED. No part of this work covered by the copyright herein may be reproduced, transmitted, stored, or used in any form or by any means graphic, electronic, or mechanical, including but not limited to photocopying, recording, scanning, digitizing, taping, Web distribution, information networks, or information storage and retrieval systems, except as permitted under Section 107 or 108 of the 1976 United States Copyright Act, without the prior written permission of the publisher.

For product information and technology assistance, contact us at
Cengage Learning Customer & Sales Support, 1-800-354-9706
For permission to use material from this text or product,
submit all requests online at **www.cengage.com/permissions**.
Further permissions questions can be e-mailed to
permissionrequest@cengage.com

CPT copyright 2012 American Medical Association. All rights reserved. CPT is a registered trademark of the American Medical Association. Applicable FARS/DFARS Restrictions Apply to Government Use. Fee schedules, relative value units, conversion factors and/or related components are not assigned by the AMA, are not part of CPT, and the AMA is not recommending their use. The AMA does not directly or indirectly practice medicine or dispense medical services. The AMA assumes no liability for data contained or not contained herein.

Library of Congress Control Number: 2012936567

ISBN-13: 978-1-111-64100-9

ISBN-10: 1-111-64100-5

Delmar
5 Maxwell Drive
Clifton Park, NY 12065-2919
USA

Cengage Learning is a leading provider of customized learning solutions with office locations around the globe, including Singapore, the United Kingdom, Australia, Mexico, Brazil, and Japan. Locate your local office at: **international.cengage.com/region**

Cengage Learning products are represented in Canada by Nelson Education, Ltd.

To learn more about Delmar, visit **www.cengage.com/delmar**

Purchase any of our products at your local college store or at our preferred online store **www.cengagebrain.com**

Notice to the Reader
Publisher does not warrant or guarantee any of the products described herein or perform any independent analysis in connection with any of the product information contained herein. Publisher does not assume, and expressly disclaims, any obligation to obtain and include information other than that provided to it by the manufacturer. The reader is expressly warned to consider and adopt all safety precautions that might be indicated by the activities described herein and to avoid all potential hazards. By following the instructions contained herein, the reader willingly assumes all risks in connection with such instructions. The publisher makes no representations or warranties of any kind, including but not limited to, the warranties of fitness for particular purpose or merchantability, nor are any such representations implied with respect to the material set forth herein, and the publisher takes no responsibility with respect to such material. The publisher shall not be liable for any special, consequential, or exemplary damages resulting, in whole or part, from the readers' use of, or reliance upon, this material.

Printed in the United States of America
1 2 3 4 5 6 7 16 15 14 13 12

Contents

Preface 1
Coding and Medical Insurance Policies 2
      Conquering Coding 3
      Coding Ground Rules 3
INTRODUCTION TO *CURRENT PROCEDURAL TERMINOLOGY (CPT)* 4
Evaluation and Management Services 5
      Evaluation and Management – I (99201–99239) 7
      Evaluation and Management – II (99241–99340) 8
      Evaluation and Management – III (99341–99499) 9
Anesthesia Services (00100–01999) 10
General Surgery Rules 11
Integumentary System 13
      Integumentary System (10021–19499) 14
Musculoskeletal System 15
      Musculoskeletal System – I (20000–23929) 16
      Musculoskeletal System – II (23930–27299) 17
      Musculoskeletal System – III (27301–29999) 18
Respiratory System 19
      Respiratory System (30000–32999) 20
Cardiovascular System 21
      Cardiovascular System (33010–37999) 22
Hemic and Lymphatic—Mediastinum and Diaphragm 23
      Hemic and Lymphatic—Mediastinum and Diaphragm (38100–39599) 24
Digestive System 25
      Digestive System (40490–49999) 26
Urinary System 27
      Urinary System (50010–53899) 28
Male Genital System 29
      Male Genital System (54000–55899) 30
Intersex, Female Genital, and Maternity 31
      Intersex, Female Genital, and Maternity (55920–59899) 32
Endocrine and Nervous Systems 33
      Endocrine and Nervous Systems (60000–64999) 34
Eye and Ocular Adnexa 35
      Eye and Ocular Adnexa (65091–68899) 36
Auditory System 37
      Auditory System (69000–69990) 38
Radiology 39
      Radiology – I (70010–73725) 40
      Radiology – II (74000–76499) 41
      Radiology – III (76506–79999) 42
Pathology and Laboratory 43
      Pathology and Laboratory – I (80047–83887) 44
      Pathology and Laboratory – II (83890–86849) 45
      Pathology and Laboratory – III (86850–89398) 46
Medicine 47
      Medicine – I (90281–92700) 48
      Medicine – II (92950–96020) 49
      Medicine – III (96040–0290T) 50
HCPCS LEVEL II CODES 51
      HCPCS Level II Codes 52
Modifiers 53
      Modifiers (2012 CPT, 2012 HCPCS) 54

INTRODUCTION TO ICD-9-CM	55
Using ICD-9-CM	56
Diagnosis Coding - Quick and Dirty	56
Reasonableness Testing	57
ICD-9-CM Official Guidelines for Coding and Reporting	58
The Ten Commandments of ICD-9-CM Diagnosis Coding	63
Moving from ICD-9-CM to ICD-10-CM	64
Coding Conflicts	67
Diagnosis Coding Worksheet Instructions	68
Infectious/Parasitic Diseases – I (001–139)	69
Infectious/Parasitic Diseases – II (001–139)	70
Neoplasms - I (140–239)	71
Neoplasms - II (140–239)	72
Endocrine, Nutritional, Metabolic, Immunity Disorders - I (240–279)	73
Endocrine, Nutritional, Metabolic, Immunity Disorders - II (240–279)	74
Blood and Blood-Forming Organs - I (280–289)	75
Blood and Blood-Forming Organs - II (280–289)	76
Mental Disorders - I (290–319)	77
Mental Disorders - II (290–319)	78
Nervous System and Sense Organs - I (320–389)	79
Nervous System and Sense Organs - II (320–389)	80
Circulatory System - I (390–459)	81
Circulatory System - II (390–459)	82
Respiratory System - I (460–519)	83
Respiratory System - II (460–519)	84
Digestive System - I (520–579)	85
Digestive System - II (520–579)	86
Genitourinary System - I (580–629)	87
Genitourinary System - II (580–629)	88
Pregnancy, Childbirth, Puerperium - I (630–679)	89
Pregnancy, Childbirth, Puerperium - II (630–679)	90
Skin and Subcutaneous Tissue - I (680–709)	91
Skin and Subcutaneous Tissue - II (680–709)	92
Musculoskeletal System and Connective Tissue - I (710–739)	93
Musculoskeletal System and Connective Tissue - II (710–739)	94
Congenital Anomalies - I (740–759)	95
Congenital Anomalies - II (740–759)	96
Conditions of the Perinatal Period - I (760–779)	97
Conditions of the Perinatal Period - II (760–779)	98
Symptoms, Signs, and Ill-Defined Conditions - I (780–799)	99
Symptoms, Signs, and Ill-Defined Conditions - II (780–799)	100
Injury and Poisoning - I (800–999)	101
Injury and Poisoning - II (800–999)	102
Supplementary Classification - "V" Codes - I (V01–V91)	103
Supplementary Classification - "V" Codes - II (V01–V91)	104
Supplementary Classification - "E" Codes - I (E000–E999)	105
Supplementary Classification - "E" Codes - II (E800–E999)	106
PUTTING IT ALL TOGETHER	107
Putting It All Together—Answers and Rationales	115
EXAM QUESTIONS FOR CPT, CPT AND HCPCS, AND ICD-9-CM	119
Exam Questions for CPT	121
Answers to Exam Questions: CPT	133
Exam Questions for CPT and HCPCS	135
Answers to Exam Questions: CPT and HCPCS	147
Exam Questions for ICD-9-CM	149
Answers to Exam Questions: ICD-9-CM	159
Appendix—Selected Answers	161

How to Use the *EncoderPro.com—Expert* 59-Day Trial

With the purchase of this textbook you receive free 59-day access to *EncoderPro.com—Expert*, the powerful online medical coding solution from Ingenix®. With *EncoderPro.com*, you can simultaneously search across all three code sets.

How to Access the Free Trial

Information on how to access your 59-day trial of *EncoderPro.com* is included on the printed tear-out card bound into this textbook. Your unique user access code is also printed on the card. Be sure to check with your instructor before beginning your free trial because it will expire 59 days after your initial login.

Features and Benefits of *EncoderPro.com*

EncoderPro.com is the essential code lookup software for CPT®, ICD-9-CM, and HCPCS code sets from Ingenix®. It gives users fast searching capabilities across all code sets. EncoderPro can greatly reduce the time it takes to build or review a claim, and helps improve overall coding accuracy.

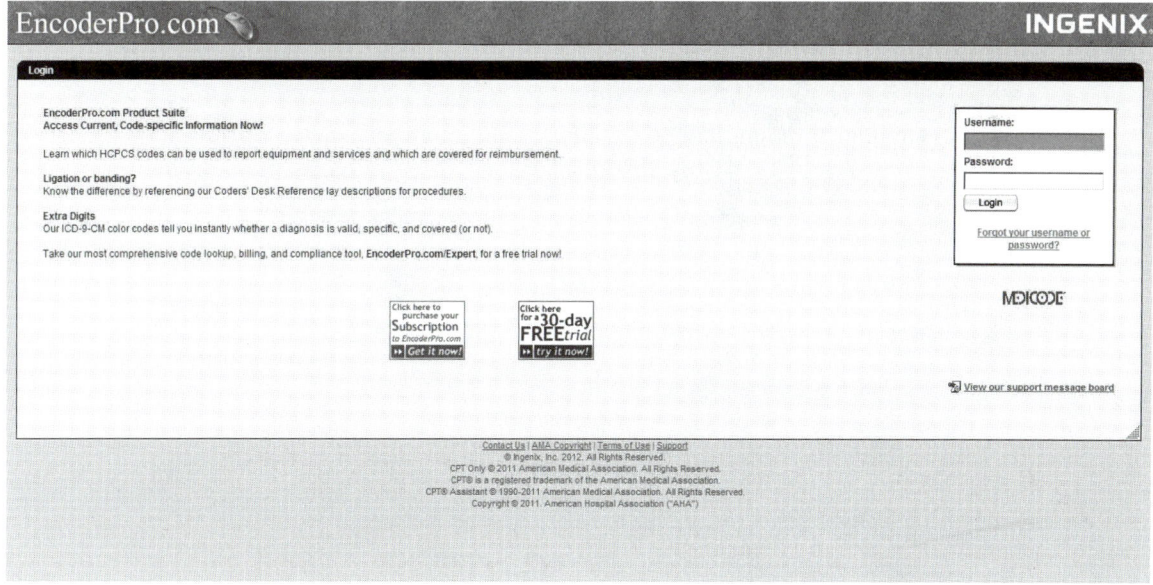

During your free trial period to *EncoderPro.com—Expert*, the following tools will be available to you:

- **Powerful Ingenix CodeLogic™ search engine.** Search all three code sets simultaneously using lay terms, acronyms, abbreviations, and even misspelled words.
- **Lay descriptions for thousands of CPT® codes.** Enhance your understanding of procedures with easy-to-understand descriptions.

v

- **Color-coded edits.** Understand whether a code carries an age or sex edit, is covered by Medicare, or contains bundled procedures.
- **ICD-10 Mapping Tool.** Crosswalk from ICD-9-CM codes to the appropriate ICD-10 code quickly and easily.
- **Great value.** Get the content from over 20 code and reference books in one powerful solution.

EncoderPro.com Video-Based Autodemo

View Ingenix's online *EncoderPro.com* video-based Autodemo at http://www.shopingenix.com by scrolling your mouse over Products and eSolutions, and clicking on the eSolution Online Demos link. Then, click on the *EncoderPro.com* link to start the Autodemo, which is approximately five minutes in length. The *EncoderPro.com* features are described and using the encoder to locate a code is demonstrated.

For more information about *EncoderPro.com*, or to become a subscriber beyond the free trial, email us at **esales@cengage.com**.

Preface

Organization of the Text

The *2012 Coding Workbook for the Physician's Office* is organized in the easiest to understand and most logical format currently available in the market for students and instructors alike. The Workbook begins with the basics, a brief foundational overview of the importance of coding and the tools necessary to succeed using this text. It is designed to be used in tandem with any main textbook or as a supplemental study material.

The Workbook begins with coding scenarios for Current Procedural Terminology (CPT), utilizing E/M codes and is broken down by body system and then by service performed. The CPT scenarios are followed by HCPCS Level II and CPT and HCPCS Modifiers coding exercises. The bulk of the workbook is comprised of ICD-9-CM and ICD-10-CM coding scenarios. The workbook is concluded with case studies, "Putting It All Together," where students can review a case study and provide proper codes based on the practice they've had using the Workbook. Answers to the case studies are provided in the back of the Workbook.

In the final preparation for students, the Workbook offers exam questions for CPT, CPT and HCPCS, ICD-9-CM. Selected answers from coding exercises are also provided in the Workbook to enhance student comprehension.

New to 2012 Coding Workbook for the Physician's Office

As 2013 approaches so too does the shift to using ICD-10-CM in medical coding. In anticipation of this industry change, the 2012 Coding Workbook has included a chapter entitled "Moving from ICD-9-CM to ICD-10-CM." This chapter provides students with an overview of the major changes that medical coding will be facing in October 2013 and challenges students to start coding with ICD-10-CM. Also, "Putting it all Together" now included a column for ICD-10-CM codes in the answers.

In addition to the new chapter on ICD-10-CM, a secondary answer column has been provided next to the ICD-9-CM answers. All of the coding scenarios have been updated to be applicable with ICD-10-CM coding guidelines. Students will not only have the benefit of learning to code with the ICD-9-CM system, but also supplement their practice and enhance their knowledge with ICD-10-CM codes. This significant contribution to the *2011 Coding Workbook for the Physician's Office*, updated for 2012, embraces the future of coding in the same easy-to-understand and logical format that has been a success since its first publication!

Supplement Package

For the Student

- 59-Day Free Trial of Ingenix's Encoder Pro is provided as a bind-in card in the back of the Workbook. This software will allow you to look up ICD-9-CM, ICD-10-CM, CPT, and HCPCS Level II codes quickly and accurately across all code sets.

For the Instructor

- The Instructor's Manual is housed online at the Instructor Companion Web site found at www.cengagebrain.com. It serves as an instructional resource and provides answers to coding exercises and test questions for content reinforcement.

- AAPC CEU approval is granted after candidates successfully pass the 30-question exam posted on Delmar Cengage Learning's online companion web site. For more information please see the back page of the Workbook.

Coding and Medical Insurance Policies

Coding can be significant in receiving, and keeping, payment for medical services. One publication says that coding makes a 25% greater or lesser difference in payment. It is the insurance policy language that defines payable benefits. Beginning coders may ask, "What code do I use to get paid?" A patient, not receiving payment, may say that the doctor reported the "wrong" code. The answer for both situations is clear. You always use the correct code.

Doctors find coding confusing. They may do a new service that does not have a specific code. Do we report it with an existing code number? Sometimes the procedure is not really new, but the doctor uses a new technique or technology. Medicare, the Blues, or another payer may notify the doctors to report these services under another code. However, without specific instructions to call the service something different, you should report it under the "unlisted procedure" code. The "Instructions for Use of the CPT Book" emphasize this point by stating, "Do not select a CPT code that merely approximates the service provided. If no such procedure or service exists, then report the service using the appropriate unlisted procedure or service code." The insurer can decide to pay or reject the claim, based on the policy coverage.

Perhaps a new code is now available for a recently developed procedure. Unfortunately, the service may be too new to appear on the insurance policy benefit list and so the payer rejects the claim. The doctor now wonders if you should code it with last year's code. You may decide to make the change after offering explanations to the irate patient who now has a large, unexpected bill. In these no-win situations, it may seem easier to recode and rebill the service. Don't do it. Resist that temptation. The medical record does not support any code but the correct one.

Insurers match the claims with their benefit schedule. Medicare pays for only a few preventive services. Religious organizations may have policies that do not cover sterilizations or abortions. Payers then send the doctor or policyholder the specified payment or a rejection. If you change the code to make the service payable, it is fraud. Also, a service may not be payable for the given diagnosis. Suppose the doctor sees a patient for bronchitis and notices that it is time to repeat the electrocardiogram, as the patient has a family history of heart disease. If the office bills the ECG with the diagnosis of bronchitis, the payer probably will reject the service. Taking an ECG is not a standard procedure for bronchitis. It is correct to report the office visit for bronchitis and the family history of heart disease for the ECG.

Some situations are less clear. No insurer would deny a person the reconstruction of his nose following a serious auto accident, a fall from a horse, or a similar incident. What if the injury occurred ten years ago? Should the auto insurer, the owner of the stable, or the patient's own insurance pay the doctor's bill? Is the patient's health insurance primary, and expected to pay first before the other insurers? All these health insurance payment problems do not affect the determination of the correct diagnosis and procedure codes.

Medicare and private insurance are separate programs. Medicare's coding rules work, and the Health Insurance Portability and Accountability Act (HIPAA) requires insurers to adopt the government-approved coding specifications of Medicare and Medicaid. If you work for a pediatrician, becoming aware of Medicare rules may be difficult. Pay close attention to payer bulletins and the information on coding distributed at their seminars and workshops. Many private organizations and medical specialty societies offer coding workshops. Try to attend one each year, and always end the year with the purchase of new coding references.

Conquering Coding

You may be surprised how much experience you have with coding. You use it every day. From social security, telephone, and credit card numbers, to thermometers and cable television selectors, numbers that represent words surround us. If you see $1.00, you think "one dollar." Even without a description or explanation, you probably recognize 1-800-555-1212.

Our present diagnosis coding system is ICD-9-CM, the *International Classification of Diseases, Ninth Revision, Clinical Modification*. Disease coding systems began in the late 1800s and identified the causes of death. The ICD system is now used worldwide to record the incidence of disease. Many ICD-9-CM reference books include this history. Take the time to read this fascinating summary of disease recording. ICD-9-CM is a three-volume reference, available from many sources at prices ranging from $19.95 to almost $200.00.

The American Medical Association (AMA) developed the procedure or service coding reference, *Current Procedural Terminology* or *CPT®*. This single volume reference is available from many sources, but the AMA carefully protects the copyright and printing of CPT.

The Health Care Financing Administration (HCFA), now named the Centers for Medicare and Medicaid Services (CMS), the agency responsible for Medicare and Medicaid, recognized that many medical services were not physician services. To report, pay, and monitor ambulance services, medical equipment, and supplies, another set of codes was needed. This system is called the *Healthcare Common Procedure Coding System* or *HCPCS* (pronounced "hick-picks"). HCPCS has two levels of codes, usually indicated by Roman numerals. The Level I codes are the CPT codes, five digit, all numeric codes. Level II codes have a letter followed by four numbers. The Level III codes, or "local" codes, were eliminated with the implementation of the HIPAA standardized code sets in October 2003.

Coding determines the appropriateness of treatment and the medical necessity for a service. Insurers compile statistics on the frequency of a service, sometimes identifying "abused" procedures. They state that many doctors do C-sections for their own convenience rather than patient need, for example. Monitoring the codes billed, Michigan Blue Shield found a physician who did almost half the endoscopic procedures reported in one year. A Medicaid program discovered a doctor who reported over 400 house calls in one day. The payers, like you, found these data unbelievable, audited the physicians, and recovered the overpayments.

Coding Ground Rules

    I.   Keep your coding references current. Purchase new books each year.

   II.   Know the coding rules and apply them properly.

  III.   Code only what the documentation supports.

  IV.   Match the diagnosis code with the procedure code. They must be "reasonable."

   V.   Review and update all charge tickets, computer files, and encounter forms annually.

INTRODUCTION TO *CURRENT PROCEDURAL TERMINOLOGY (CPT)*

The American Medical Association (AMA) released the first edition of *Current Procedural Terminology (CPT)* in 1966. It was similar to a coding system developed ten years earlier by the California Medical Association (CMA) called the *California Relative Value System (CRVS)*. These codes were based on a four-digit system. In 1970, the AMA released the Second Edition of CPT, adding a fifth digit to make services more specific. The Third Edition was printed in 1973 and the Fourth Edition in 1977. Also, during this time, many insurance companies developed their own coding systems. Some payers used these coding systems internally, and others required the doctor use these special codes to report services to that insurer.

By 1983, a government study identified over 120 different procedure-coding systems. It was impossible to match services in all these different coding systems, so the government mandated a standard coding system for Medicare and Medicaid. Beginning in 1984, the government required physicians to report all services in HCPCS for all Medicare and Medicaid claims. Also in 1984, the AMA modified the name of CPT and began including the year in the title.

CPT-1992 changed all the "visit" services, such as office calls, hospital care, and nursing home visits, to "evaluation and management" services. In spite of many articles in medical publications, seminars, and newsletters, some physicians still have trouble determining the exact level of care to use for a patient. While deciding the correct level of service is the responsibility of the physician, not the medical assistant or biller, we will explore these codes in the worksheets. Medicare required this change as part of their implementation of the Resource Based Relative Value Scale (RBRVS) mandated by Congress to reform the Medicare payment structure.

The present edition of CPT contains over 7,500 different descriptions of services. The AMA protects these codes and descriptions by a copyright. Look at the introductory pages of the current edition. They give credit to the CPT Panel and Advisory Committees responsible for developing these codes. The Table of Contents shows the organization of the references. Note that the largest section, as you would expect, is the Surgery listing. Appendix B summarizes the code changes since the last edition. This list identifies the codes you must update in your computer or on office documents. Some CPT vendors and the AMA have editions with color-coded pages, color keys, and thumb-indexed pages to make it easier to use. Their terminology and illustration sections can provide guidance with unfamiliar terms. The CPT Index is not complete, but it can help you search for new codes.

Most successful projects start at the beginning. Look at the CPT Introduction. Many of the higher numbered codes, the E/M (evaluation and management) services, appear first since most physicians do these services. Any doctor can report a code from any section, if that is the service performed. However, reasonableness must be tested. Would a podiatrist perform neurosurgery? Not likely, but it could appear that way if you transpose digits in the procedure code. Later, we will work with a worksheet that looks at reasonable code matching. The terminology format, with the stem of the procedure before the semicolon, saves space and makes the page easier to read. This code layout is standard in the CPT, HCPCS, and ICD-9-CM references.

Coding guidelines appear in each CPT section. You must read these carefully to select the correct codes in this workbook. Procedure descriptions may be misleading if you have not read the rules. We will review the "separate procedures" in the surgery section. The "modifiers" do just that; they modify or change a service. They are so important that all modifiers are listed in CPT Appendix A. Complete your reading of the Introduction and review any terminology and anatomy pages. Now you are ready to start the worksheets.

Evaluation and Management Services

The first three worksheets cover the basic medical visit services provided by almost every health care professional. These are the Evaluation and Management (E/M) codes. The service descriptions are complete, but confusing. An understanding of terms is critical to accurate interpretation of the services. You must read the CPT definitions of commonly used terms carefully. If you are responsible for billing and have obsolete codes or descriptions on the office encounter forms, change them immediately. You may find an old code or modifier in your computer system. Delete them only after making certain you do not need them for statistical use. Contact the vendor of your computer system or software to find the correct procedure for handling obsolete codes and modifiers.

There are three to five levels of many E/M codes. Encounter forms may have a cell labeled "New Patient" and code 99201 listed with the description "Level 1." The guidelines also advise you that the descriptions vary for all Level 1 codes. As you review the instructions, look at the codes used for illustration. The presenting problems, time, and face-to-face clarifications are essential components of the service descriptions. Review the instructions on selecting a level of E/M service with the doctors and other professionals so that the documentation in the patient's medical record matches the service level reported.

CPT Appendix C provides some clinical examples for each level of service. These are identified by specialty and may help you to select the correct code. Do not read anything into the case study that is not there. If we assumed that the patient was blind, obese, or had another complicating problem, the level of service might change. Base your interpretation on the information provided, and nothing else.

Remember our earlier reference to policy benefits deciding whether a code would result in payment? The same rules affect modifiers. Medicare allows the modifier -21, prolonged E/M service, when applied to only the high-level codes. Other payers may not honor or may have special rules for using a specific modifier.

Following the guidelines section, CPT begins with the E/M codes. You will find explanatory information throughout the section. You must read these instructions. Many worksheet items use this additional material. The reformatted visit codes on the next page show the similarities and contrasts for these services. Some criteria are consistent for most codes. New patient services require all three key components: history, examination, and medical decision making. Established patient services need two of the three key components. The wording of the paragraph on counseling and coordination of care is consistent throughout the E/M codes.

This section, the visit codes, may be the most complex in CPT. From here it will become easier. Again, review the guidelines and other instructions carefully, as they explain the components of each code. Code the worksheets of E/M encounters, described in terms used by physicians, not the CPT committee. You may not agree with the level of the code listed on the answer sheet, but your choice should be from the same group of codes. Aren't we glad that choosing the appropriate level of E/M codes is the responsibility of the doctor and not the coders? However, your knowledge of these codes can help the provider choose the appropriate code for the service.

In 1995, the AMA and HCFA released the documentation standards for E/M services. These described the components of the medical history and the number of body areas and organ systems that the doctor must examine and document for each level of service. In 1997, HCFA clarified this list by identifying the mandatory elements of the exam. The doctor supports a detailed exam (99203) by documenting twelve to seventeen exam items. The complexity of medical decision making is also explained. Be certain there is a copy of these criteria in your office so anyone creating medical records can follow these guidelines. All payers should accept this documentation standard, and the AMA may include it in future editions of CPT.

When the first three E/M services are placed next to each other, it is easier to see the similarities and differences between the codes:

New Patient - 99201	**New Patient - 99202**	**New Patient - 99203**
Office or other outpatient visit for the evaluation and management of a new patient, which requires these three key components:	Office or other outpatient visit for the evaluation and management of a new patient, which requires these three key components:	Office or other outpatient visit for the evaluation and management of a new patient, which requires these three key components:
• a problem-focused history;	• an expanded problem-focused history;	• a detailed history;
• a problem-focused examination; and	• an expanded problem-focused examination; and	• a detailed examination; and
• straightforward medical decision making.	• straightforward medical decision making.	• medical decision making of low complexity.
Counseling and/or coordination of care with other providers or agencies are provided consistent with the nature of the problem(s) and the patient's and/or family's needs.	Counseling and/or coordination of care with other providers or agencies are provided consistent with the nature of the problem(s) and the patient's and/or family's needs.	Counseling and/or coordination of care with other providers or agencies are provided consistent with the nature of the problem(s) and the patient's and/or family's needs.
Usually, the presenting problem(s) are self-limited or minor. Physicians typically spend 10 minutes face-to-face with the patient and/or family.	Usually, the presenting problem(s) are of low to moderate severity. Physicians typically spend 20 minutes face-to-face with the patient and/or family.	Usually, the presenting problem(s) are of moderate severity. Physicians typically spend 30 minutes face-to-face with the patient and/or family.

Name _____

Evaluation and Management – I (99201–99239)

2012 CPT Codes

These codes cover office and outpatient visits, hospital daily visits, and medical services for patients in hospital observation units. Most physicians use visit codes, and sometimes they make up over 90% of the services performed by a physician.

Remember, some E/M services may require modifiers.

1. Discussion of medications with patient's family just before patient left the observation unit *[discharge]* — 99217
2. Hospital visit, will discharge patient tomorrow *[subsequent]* — 99231
3. First visit; multiple complaints; meds for diabetes, arthritis, and hypertension reviewed and changed, as patient has rash secondary to present combination; also fulgurated wart on left ring finger *[new patient]* _____
4. Visit with nurse to verify proper use of inhaler _____
5. Six-month follow-up visit for patient # 3 above _____
6. First day in observation unit, patient collapsed at shopping mall and continues to have an irregular heartbeat _____
7. Admission to hospital for Boy Scout with severe poison ivy _____
8. Initial office visit for child with chicken pox _____
9. Eight-year-old girl seen again for severe sore throat and fatigue _____
10. Admission to ICU for 72-year-old male with massive cerebral hemorrhage, respiratory failure, and coma _____
11. Hospital visit for patient with severe reaction (rash, vomiting) to x-ray study dye, medication prescribed _____
12. Comprehensive follow-up counseling visit, emotionally upset over child's behavior and marital problems, 3:15 to 4:00 p.m. _____
13. Forty-eight-year-old male admitted to hospital for chest pain and discharged the same day when all diagnostic studies were within normal limits _____
14. Spent 20 minutes reviewing improving lab work and discussing results. Will reduce meds, may discharge from observation tomorrow _____

Name _____

Evaluation and Management – II (99241–99340)

2012 CPT Codes

Consultations occur when one physician or provider requests the OPINION of another physician or provider. The consultant may perform tests to establish the opinion or may initiate treatment, but the patient remains under the care of the requesting physician. If the consulting physician assumes part or all the care of the patient, it is a referral and not a consultation. A surgeon is usually not a consultant but is expected to take care of the patient's problem. The term "consultation" is sometimes misused, as when the patient "consults" with the doctor. Consultation codes have two subcategories: office/outpatient and inpatient. Medicare stopped paying consultation codes in 2010, citing misuse. There are also codes for Emergency Services, Critical Care, Nursing Facility Services, as well as Domiciliary, Rest Home, and Custodial Care Services.

1. Office consult for high school senior with a knee injury that occurred during the homecoming game _____

2. Comprehensive admission service for the transfer of a psychotic patient from an acute care hospital to a psychiatric residential treatment center _____

3. Initial hospital consult for male diabetic, back surgery 3 days ago; now has a severe urinary tract infection, emergency procedure scheduled for this afternoon _____

4. One hour in ER with 3-year-old attacked by a pit bull, found unconscious with bruises and scrapes, no suturing required _____

5. Annual nursing facility visit _____

6. Brief inpatient consult to rule out abscessed tooth in post-delivery female _____

7. ICU consult for female with cardiac arrest during gallbladder surgery, now in a coma _____

8. Office consultation for teenager with severe acne _____

9. Visit to home for the developmentally disabled to see a new patient with recent onset of swelling in hands and feet _____

10. Constant attendance, 1.5 hours critical care in ICU, 15-year-old male, comatose after diving accident _____

11. Office consult for 58-year-old with Alzheimer's and previous stroke, now combative and incontinent _____

12. One-hour discussion with family of an elderly patient being discharged from rehabilitation facility to son's home for aftercare _____

13. Seen in critical care unit, detailed history/exam, will transfer to surgeon if not improved in 24 hours _____

14. Follow-up skilled nursing facility visit for patient with recent onset of mini-strokes (30 minutes) _____

15. Contact with family and staff of assisted living facility revising care plan based on recent laboratory studies (July: 22 minutes) _____

16. Revisit to Alzheimer's patient in foster care home who now has a urinary tract infection _____

Name _____

Evaluation and Management – III (99341–99499)

2012 CPT Codes

These codes are used to report Home Services, Prolonged Services, Physician Standby Services, Case Management, Team conferences, Care plan oversight, Preventive Medicine, Newborn/Infant Services, and Miscellaneous care. They cover special or preventive services that may be excluded under some insurance policies. Be certain the codes you report accurately reflect the services performed so the insurer can appropriately pay or reject the claim. Some services may be payable only for certain diagnoses or in specified locations.

1. Follow-up house call for child recovering from flu _____

2. Extended follow-up in NICU, unstable 2-month-old infant _____

3. Admission of premature newborn to NICU _____

4. Injured 18-month-old infant transported to Children's Hospital, pediatrician in attendance for 55-minute trip   99060
   99082

5. One-hour conference at day-care center with psychologist, nurse, and geriatric assessment staff, pending transfer of patient to long-term care facility _____

6. Forty-five minutes of Internet evaluations over the weekend with an established patient not seen in the past month but now threatening suicide _____

7. Initial exam of infant born at home _____

8. NICU visit, 5-day-old infant now weighing 4,200 grams, will transfer to nursery tomorrow _____

9. New patient, annual exam for pilot, age 47 _____

10. Following an EPF visit (99282) in the ER for a 90-year-old patient, the physician spent another hour with the patient's spouse and children contacting long-term care facilities and a geriatric physician to develop a plan of care for the patient _____

11. Standby services (35 minutes) required for cesarean/high-risk delivery _____

12. Counseling on risk factors, sexually active 14-year-old female, 45 minutes _____

13. Preschool exam for 5-year-old seen since infancy _____

14. Services for the month of June (25 minutes) supervising the hospice team for care of terminally ill cancer patient, patient not seen _____

15. Initial home visit to discuss care options with family of an 88-year-old disabled stroke patient, 1 hour _____

16. In-office initial management and monitoring of 47-year-old male on Coumadin, 9 INR tests and subsequent dosage adjustment, 2nd quarter _____

Anesthesia Services (00100–01999)

2012 CPT Codes

Physicians who are not anesthesiologists may report anesthesia services. A doctor may be responsible for the anesthesia when a partner performs a surgical procedure. Some large practices have their own surgery room, performing the same procedures in the office that they would do in the hospital outpatient surgicenter. In some cases, an anesthesiologist may not be available. Medical billers should become familiar with these codes and the rules for using them. These services may be a significant part of your coding work in the future.

Anesthesia uses some special modifiers to indicate the patient's condition, P1 through P6, and some of the usual CPT modifiers. There are also some 99xxx codes that you bill along with the regular anesthesia service when there are special qualifying circumstances. Keep these special rules in mind as you complete the worksheet.

The descriptions do not specify anesthesia, but all answers should come from this section. Watch for procedures that need a modifier or multiple codes.

1. Cervical diagnostic discography injection _____
2. Abdominal repair, hernia of the diaphragm _____
3. Delivery of twins, no C-section _____
4. Radiation therapy requiring general anesthesia _____
5. Total joint replacement, left ankle, for severe arthritis _____
6. Open reduction, fracture right distal humerus _____
7. Burr holes, critical newborn infant _____
8. Dual chamber transvenous pacemaker insertion _____
9. Rhinoplasty, correction of deviated septum _____
10. Mid-thigh amputation, right leg _____
11. Harrington rod implant, spinal cord biopsy _____
12. Rectal endoscopy with biopsy _____
13. Insert umbrella filter, inferior vena cava _____
14. Pectus excavatum repair, 4-year-old male _____
15. Arthroscopy, right shoulder _____

General Surgery Rules

Surgical procedures on the integumentary system begin the extensive surgery section. CPT provides important guidelines for all surgeries. Review them carefully. Then consider the information below as you review the worksheet items.

1. Necessary medical care for diagnostic surgery may be reported separately. Non-diagnostic surgical services include concurrent medical care by the operating surgeon. Other physicians may report medical care that is unrelated to the surgical service. Example: A patient undergoing gallbladder surgery is followed by an internist for chronic emphysema. The internist is paid for the medical care as it is not related to the surgical service. Medicare has comprehensive tables identifying, by procedure code, the days of medical care included in a surgical service. Other insurers may use the same list or have similar restrictions.

2. Surgical services usually include any local anesthesia administered by the operating surgeon.

3. The payment for the surgery includes all related supplies. The doctor may bill for supplies only if they exceed what is usually required for that service. Insurers may refuse to pay for any additional supplies provided by the surgeon. If the surgery is done in the hospital setting, either inpatient or outpatient, payers assume the hospital provided all the necessary supplies.

4. The subsection information contains the special instructions for using a particular range of codes. In some cases, this vital information may appear on the previous page. Always, after you find the code you seek, review the previous page or two for any special rules related to this coding section.

5. A service that is usually part of another service may, on occasion, be reported as the primary surgery. These codes appear throughout CPT and the description ends with "(separate procedure)." If you perform a service with the (separate procedure) notation, report that service if it is the ONLY service performed or is unrelated to the other procedures or services performed. Use the modifier –59, Distinct Procedural Service, to indicate this service is unrelated to the other procedures or services reported. This is a rule many doctors and billers find confusing.

6. Surgical destruction is usually included in the primary procedure.

7. Use the unlisted procedure code at the end of each surgery section when there is no code for the service performed. New procedures are reported with these codes until a specific code is assigned. If the service involves a new technique for an established procedure, you would usually report the service with the existing code unless the technique is specified in the description. Note that all unlisted procedure codes end in "9" and many end in "99." Remember, whenever you report these unlisted services, you will need to make the operative notes available or provide a complete description of the service.

8. The special report is similar to the unlisted procedure. Again, you must explain the service completely. Documentation must be sent with the claim. These claims may not be accepted electronically as they require attachments. Some payers have a fax line to receive the required documentation for electronic claims.

9. Some of the CPT surgery modifiers may be listed in the guidelines of the surgery section. All CPT modifiers appear in Appendix A.

10. Some complications may be reported in addition to the surgery using the modifier –22 and a detailed explanation. Medicare will usually reject any medical care billed by the surgeon during the specified postoperative period. To get paid, the surgeon must establish that the medical care rendered is not part of the usual postoperative care for the previous surgery.

11. Modifiers –54, –53, and –56 cover situations where the surgeon does not provide all the medical care related to the surgery. Physicians other than the surgeon may provide and be paid for medical care related to the surgery if the surgeon indicates his service does not include the preoperative or postoperative medical care.

12. Sometimes the doctor performs multiple procedures. If the surgery is a bilateral carpal tunnel release, you may be instructed by the payer to report the code and the modifier –50 or to report two identical lines, one with modifier –RT and the other with modifier –LT. Suppose the patient has gallbladder surgery and the doctor also removes nevi from the neck and left thigh, and a basal cell CA of the scalp. You would report the major procedure on the first line, the basal cell CA on the second line, and the nevi on subsequent lines in the order of diminishing significance. The modifier –51 would be used on all but the first service line. Exception: See 14 below. Also, each service line must show the appropriate diagnosis code reference number.

13. Therapeutic surgery includes all related medical care. The modifier –24 is used when the surgeon performs a separate, postoperative medical service unrelated to the surgical procedure. Example: A patient had a surgery last week but now visits the surgeon's office for an acute asthma attack. If the asthma is unrelated to the surgery, the office visit may be billed as a separate service with modifier –24.

14. Some multiple surgical procedures must be reported without modifier –51. These are the "add on" codes, identified in CPT Appendix D. Because these codes are added on to the reporting of another code, they can never be used alone. When printing paper claim forms, be sure that these codes do not roll over to be the only service on another claim form.

15. CPT Appendix E lists the CPT codes that are not "add on" codes but do not require the modifier –51. Codes such as 20975 (electrical stimulation to aid bone healing, invasive, operative) or 31500 (intubation, endotracheal, emergency procedure) are billable but may be related to another reported service. Watch this Appendix closely if you perform these services, as this list is updated yearly. Medicare rejects these codes as incorrectly reported if modifier –51 is attached.

Modifiers increase in importance every year. Each new edition of CPT and HCPCS bring changes in the familiar ones and new modifiers. Be certain you review the modifier sections when you look for changes in procedure codes.

Medicare and most other payers reject "unbundling," the reporting of multiple services when one code includes all procedures. When physicians code from a list, they may miss a code that contains multiple services. Encounter forms or coding sheets may state:

51840	Marshall-Marchetti
58150	Abdominal Hysterectomy
58700	Salpingectomy(ies)
58940	Oophorectomy(ies)

Turn to code 58150. The description includes codes 58700 and 58940. Suppose the patient with the abdominal hysterectomy also had a Marshall-Marchetti-type procedure. The correct code, 58152, contains all the procedures listed above. The CMS rebundling list is called the "Correct Coding Initiative" or CCI and is revised quarterly. Many insurance carriers implement these policies as soon as CMS releases them.

Caution: The CPT worksheets may require multiple procedure codes, a modifier, or the reporting of quantity. Any time the CPT code says "each," you need to report a quantity, even if it is only one. As you complete the worksheets, pronounce the terms. You can increase your vocabulary as you expand your coding skills.

Integumentary System

These codes include procedures on the skin, subcutaneous and accessory structures, nail, and breast. They cover the removal of lesions, suturing, plastic repairs, burn treatment, and other surgeries. Read the embedded instructions immediately under the headings "Removal of Skin Tags" and "Shaving of Epidermal or Dermal Lesions." Would we report suturing with the shaving of a dermal lesion? No, because the notation states that "the wound does not require suture closure."

Look at CPT's Rule 2 for Repair (Closure) when repairing multiple lacerations. Add together the length of all wounds in the same classification and report the total as a single item. This rule does not apply to excising multiple lesions, as each is reported individually. A ruler with both inches and centimeters will help you report the correct codes for lesions and suturing.

Before beginning the worksheets, look at the codes and read the text of the entire integumentary section. You may wish to have a medical dictionary and anatomy reference handy. Benign lesions are listed before malignant; suturing is simple, intermediate, and complex; and the miscellaneous categories list services that do not fit into other sections. The integumentary system ends with procedures on the breast.

Note: Watch for worksheet items requiring a modifier, quantity, or multiple codes.

Name _____

Integumentary System (10021–19499)

2012 CPT Codes   15775-15776

1. Hair transplant, 21 punch grafts — 15776
2. Removal of 8 skin tags from left forearm
3. Implant Norplant contraceptive capsules
4. Simple blepharoplasty, right upper lid
5. Reclosure, 3 surgical wounds
6. Debridement of skin and subcutaneous tissue, left forearm
7. Permanent removal distal half, left great toenail
8. Full thickness graft 2 × 5 cm, left cheek
9. Simple right shoulder biopsy, single skin lesion
10. Adjacent tissue transfer, trunk, 8 sq cm
11. Laser destruction, benign 2 cm facial lesion
12. Excision/Z-plasty repair, 11 sq cm forehead lesion
13. Aspiration, breast cyst, right
14. Burn site preparation of back, 4%, 9-year-old female
15. Wound suture, 3/4" right hand, 1/2" left foot
16. Breast reduction, left
17. Excision, simple repair, right axillary hidradenitis
18. Xenograft, left thigh, 4 × 8 cm
19. Excise malignant 1/2" lesion, neck
20. I&D hematoma, left hand
21. Major debridement of partial thickness burns, both legs
22. Mohs' technique, 7 tissue blocks, abdomen
23. Leg Fx, open, debride left thigh, remove gravel, bone spicules
24. Split autograft, back (2% body area), 2-year-old male
25. Lipectomy, right buttock

Musculoskeletal System

Three worksheets on the musculoskeletal system cover the largest unit in the surgery section. They describe procedures on the supporting structures of the body such as bone, muscle, and tendon. The first worksheet includes trauma, excision/removal, replantation, grafting, the head, neck and thorax, spine, abdomen, and shoulder. The second worksheet has procedures on the arm, hand and fingers, and pelvis and hip joint. The third involves services on the femur, knee, leg, ankle, and foot, and concludes with casting, strapping, and arthroscopy.

The many rules and definitions appearing within the chapter give specific instructions on coding. Note that the service includes the first cast or traction device. This information is repeated at the start of the casting section. There are also modifiers to identify the service as right or left, and ones that identify specific digits.

Some doctors use the terms "closed" and "open" to describe the fracture rather than the treatment. If you believe this is happening in your office, talk to the doctor and get this clarified before billing the service.

The musculoskeletal system is arranged by body site, from the top down, from the center out. After the general procedures, it is organized:

1. Head
2. Neck and thorax
3. Back and flank
4. Spine
5. Abdomen
6. Shoulder
7. Humerus and elbow
8. Forearm and wrist
9. Hand and fingers
10. Pelvis and hip joint
11. Femur and knee joint
12. Leg and ankle joint
13. Foot and toes
14. Casts and Strapping

Each body site section follows this organization:

1. Incision
2. Excision
3. Introduction or removal
4. Repair, revision, reconstruction
5. Fracture and/or dislocation
6. Manipulation
7. Arthrodesis
8. Amputation
9. Miscellaneous

Note how many worksheet items in the musculoskeletal section contain the diagnosis. Watch for items that need multiple procedure codes; right, left, finger, and toe modifiers; or quantity specified.

Musculoskeletal System – I (20000–23929)

2012 CPT Codes

1. Percutaneous needle biopsy, right deltoid muscle
2. Partial acromionectomy, left
3. Wick monitoring, muscle compartment syndrome, right leg
4. Four segment kyphectomy
5. Injection service for left TMJ arthrogram
6. LeFort II reconstruction, 2 autografts
7. Removal of deep right shoulder prosthesis for replacement
8. Fracture of mandible, dental fixation, closed
9. Maxillectomy, intra-extra oral osteotomy, for cyst
10. Radical sternal resection with major bone graft for osteomyelitis (2 codes)
11. Remove external wire fixation under anesthesia
12. Treat open fractures, 2 thoracic vertebrae
13. Right shoulder arthrodesis, no graft
14. Care of simple nasal fracture, no manipulation or stabilization
15. Right total shoulder
16. Reattachment of total amputation of right thumb tip
17. Anterior osteotomy, discectomy, 2 thoracic vertebrae (2 codes)
18. Medrol injection, right hip
19. Exploratory arthrotomy, left A-C joint
20. Open treatment blowout fracture, right orbit
21. Microvascular anastomosis, osteocutaneous flap, left great toe
22. Custom prosthesis preparation, left ear
23. Explore right chest, multiple gunshot wounds
24. Incise/drain deep soft tissue, osteomyelitic abscess, left buttock
25. Exploration of fusion, lumbar spine

Name _____

Musculoskeletal System – II (23930–27299)

2012 CPT Codes

1. Open repair of left Dupuytren's contracture _____
2. Hypothenar opponensplasty, right _____
3. Open Bennett fracture with internal fixation, left _____
4. Secondary flexor repair and graft, right no man's land _____
5. Synovial biopsy of right elbow by arthrotomy _____
6. Manipulation lunate dislocation, closed _____
7. Darrach procedure, left _____
8. Decompression fasciotomy, extensor, left wrist _____
9. Fx left olecranon, internal fixation, open treatment _____
10. Right Z-plasty fasciectomy with release of 3rd and 4th IP joints (multiple codes) _____
11. Repair nonunion of left radius without graft _____
12. Treatment of traumatic left hip dislocation, no anesthesia _____
13. Flap repair, syndactyly, right 4th web space _____
14. Removal of recurrent ganglion, left wrist _____
15. Transmetacarpal reamputation, left first finger _____
16. Subfascial soft tissue biopsy, right forearm _____
17. Manipulation with pin, left epicondylar fracture _____
18. Closed manipulation MP dislocation left 4th finger, with anesthesia _____
19. Saucerization distal phalanx, left ring finger _____
20. Total hip replacement, right _____
21. Remove implant, revise arthroplasty, left wrist _____
22. Opposition fusion and graft, left thumb _____
23. Microvascular toe-to-hand transfer 2nd and 3rd toe to previous bone graft, left hand _____
24. Right femur, epiphyseal arrest by stapling _____
25. Reinsert ruptured left distal triceps tendon with graft _____

Name _____

Musculoskeletal System – III (27301–29999)

2012 CPT Codes

1. Right shoulder arthroscopy with lysis of adhesions _____
2. Phalangectomy, left third toe _____
3. Exploration with synovial biopsy by arthrotomy, left knee _____
4. Release of left tarsal tunnel _____
5. Left knee arthroscopy, sewing needle removed _____
6. Fracture right medial malleolus, closed, no manipulation _____
7. Surgical correction with fixation, left patellar fracture _____
8. Gastrocnemius neurectomy, left _____
9. Heyman midtarsal capsulotomy, right _____
10. Lengthening bilateral hamstring tendons _____
11. I&D hematoma, left ankle _____
12. Repair of Risser jacket _____
13. Fracture femoral shaft, open with screws, left _____
14. Right Joplin bunion repair _____
15. Repair of severed collateral ligament, right ankle _____
16. Knock-knee osteotomy, left, before closure _____
17. Lengthening, left Achilles tendon _____
18. Plantar fasciotomy, left, by arthroscopy _____
19. Goldwaite procedure for dislocating patella, right _____
20. Manipulation right trimalleolar fracture _____
21. Guillotine amputation, left tibia/fibula _____
22. Application of right long arm splint _____
23. Left sesamoid fracture, closed treatment _____
24. Revision right long leg cast, walker heel applied _____
25. Right great toe IP joint arthrodesis _____

Respiratory System

From nosebleed and tonsillectomy to removal of a lung, this section covers procedures associated with the nose, sinuses, larynx, trachea, bronchi, lungs, and pleura.

In this system, we are introduced to endoscopy. Note that when a surgical or therapeutic endoscopy is performed, the appropriate sinusotomy, diagnostic endoscopy, and inspecting all sinuses is included. This is another example of correct coding or bundling of services.

Respiratory System (30000–32999)

2012 CPT Codes

1. Partial removal, left inferior turbinate _____
2. Split cricoid laryngoplasty _____
3. Endoscopy with A&P ethmoidectomy _____
4. Closure nasoseptal perforations from cocaine use _____
5. Bronchoscopy with laser destruction of lesions _____
6. Tube thoracostomy for empyema _____
7. External arytenoidopexy _____
8. Revision of tracheostoma _____
9. Parietal pleurectomy _____
10. Intranasal antrotomy, right _____
11. Plastic repair closure of tracheostomy _____
12. Intrathoracic tracheoplasty _____
13. Tracheobronchoscopy through tracheostomy _____
14. Direct laryngoscopy with biopsy, via microscope _____
15. Surgical nasal endoscopy, polypectomy _____
16. Secondary major rhinoplasty _____
17. Removal of toy from nose, 2-year-old male, in office _____
18. Pneumonolysis with packing _____
19. Radical neck, partial laryngectomy for CA _____
20. Unilateral sinusotomy, 3 sinusus, right _____
21. Polypectomy, office surgery _____
22. Empyemectomy _____
23. Surgical endoscopy, repair sphenoid CSF leak _____
24. Thoracoscopy, with wedge resection _____
25. Puncture aspiration, left lung _____

Cardiovascular System

This section lists the surgical procedures on the vascular and cardiac systems: the heart, veins, and arteries. The instructional introductory paragraphs refer to first-, second-, and third-order vessels and vascular families and the injection procedures for arteriography.

The Society of Interventional Radiology (SIR) distributes an excellent reference explaining the family trees of the vascular system. This manual is available on their Web site:

>http://directory.sirweb.org/store/

Because surgery on the cardiovascular system usually represents major surgery, there are few codes identified as "separate procedure." Operations on the arteries and veins include the intraoperative angiogram. Aortic procedures include the sympathectomy, if performed. Diagnostic cardiac catheterization is in the Medicine section.

Review the extensive explanation of pacemaker and cardioverter-defibrillator services. Coronary bypass grafting, both venous and arterial, is complex and requires careful reading.

Caution: Watch out for worksheet item 3. Move slowly and carefully through this CPT section.

Cardiovascular System (33010–37999)

2012 CPT Codes

1. Short saphenous vein stripping, left leg _____
2. Vein graft repair, left brachial artery _____
3. Coronary bypass grafts, 1 venous and 2 arterial _____
4. Direct repair of vertebral artery aneurysm _____
5. Revision of pacemaker pocket _____
6. Percutaneous removal of broken arterial catheter fragment _____
7. Open atrial septostomy with bypass _____
8. Insertion AV sequential pacemaker and electrodes _____
9. Needle placement, left jugular vein _____
10. Removal of implanted arterial infusion pump _____
11. Pulmonary artery embolectomy without bypass _____
12. Mitral valvotomy with bypass _____
13. Cardiectomy with heart transplant _____
14. Intracatheter AV shunt for dialysis _____
15. Diagnostic arterial puncture _____
16. Cutdown venipuncture, newborn _____
17. Splenorenal bypass, synthetic graft _____
18. Percutaneous transluminal fem-pop atherectomy, left _____
19. Direct repair of ruptured splenic artery aneurysm _____
20. Intrauterine fetal transfusion _____
21. Repeat pericardiocentesis _____
22. Repair lacerated aorta with cardiopulmonary bypass _____
23. Resection with commissurotomy for infundibular stenosis _____
24. Ligation/repair patent ductus arteriosus, 19-year-old female _____
25. Patch closure of ventricular septal defect _____

Hemic and Lymphatic—Mediastinum and Diaphragm

These combined, small sections include procedures on the spleen, bone marrow, stem cell services/procedures, lymph nodes and channels, mediastinum, and diaphragm.

Compared to the cardiovascular section, this one is easy.

Note how many services are (separate procedure). These services are usually performed at the same time and setting of other major procedures and are not reported separately.

Hemic and Lymphatic—Mediastinum and Diaphragm (38100-39599)

2012 CPT Codes

1. Superficial needle biopsy of inguinal lymph node
2. Complete right axillary lymphadenectomy
3. Repair acute traumatic hernia of diaphragm
4. Insertion of thoracic duct cannula
5. Drainage of single lymph node abscess, left axilla
6. Laparoscopic splenectomy
7. Excision of deep axillary node, right
8. Radical retroperitoneal lymphadenectomy
9. Lymphangiotomy
10. Mediastinoscopy with biopsy
11. Partial splenectomy for traumatic injury
12. Superficial inguino-femoral lymphadenectomy
13. Retroperitoneal staging lymphadenectomy
14. Correct newborn diaphragmatic hernia, insert chest tube
15. Needle bone marrow biopsy
16. Suprahyoid lymphadenectomy, right
17. Eventration of paralytic diaphragm
18. Deep jugular node dissection × 3
19. Allogenic bone marrow transplant
20. Injection for lymphangiography, bilateral
21. Removal of benign neoplasm from mediastinum
22. Staging, partial pelvic lymphadenectomy
23. Excise left axillary hygroma, deep neurovascular dissection
24. Repair ruptured spleen
25. Total pelvic lymphadenectomy by laparoscope

Digestive System

This system covers procedures on the mouth, salivary glands, pharynx, adenoids, tonsils, esophagus, stomach, intestines, appendix, rectum and anus, liver, biliary tract, pancreas, abdomen, peritoneum, omentum, and hernia repair.

This diverse section contains endoscopic procedures and refers to the related radiographic guidance, supervision, and interpretation services. Remember that surgical endoscopy includes diagnostic endoscopy.

Watch for multiple codes and the items that require a modifier.

Name _____

Digestive System (40490–49999)

2012 CPT Codes

1. I&D peritonsillar abscess
2. Flexible esophagoscopy with removal of FB
3. Open Roux-en-Y bypass for obesity
4. Fredet-Ramstedt pyloromyotomy
5. Transanal hemicolectomy
6. Commando glossectomy
7. Initial inguinal hernia repair, 4-year-old male
8. Transsacral proctectomy
9. Rubber band ligature hemorrhoidectomy
10. ERCP with pancreatic duct stent
11. Stomal colonoscopy for hemorrhage
12. Upper GI endoscopy, dilate obstructed outlet
13. Staging laparotomy for Hodgkin's, with intraoperative tube jejunostomy
14. Second stage, primary bilateral cleft lip repair
15. Total arch vestibuloplasty
16. Subsequent peritoneal lavage with imaging
17. Rectal stricture dilation under general anesthesia
18. Cholecystectomy with cholangiography
19. Thoracic closure of esophagostomy
20. Flexible sigmoidoscopy for biopsy
21. Partial left lobe hepatectomy
22. Salivary gland biopsy by incision
23. Hepaticoenterostomy, by Utube
24. Removal of dental implant, left mandible
25. Plastic repair of pharynx

Urinary System

This section includes the procedures on the kidneys, ureters, bladder, and urethra and also transplant services, including the harvesting of the kidney. Urinary endoscopy and other procedures identify special bundling instructions.

Caution: Read the worksheet items carefully. Urethra and ureter can look similar in some forms of the words. Note the different codes for male and female.

One worksheet item has two possible codes. What else do you need to know to find the exact code?

Name _____

Urinary System (50010–53899)

2012 CPT Codes

1. Subsequent urethral stricture dilation, 27-year-old male _____
2. Transurethral resection of prostate _____
3. Closure of traumatic kidney wound _____
4. Infant meatotomy _____
5. Cystourethroscopy, fulguration of 1.9 cm tumor _____
6. Complete cystectomy, bilateral lymphadenectomy _____
7. Bowel anastomosis with ureterocolon conduit _____
8. Repair of ureterovisceral fistula _____
9. Needleless EMG anal sphincter _____
10. Subsequent dilation urethra, 21-year-old female, no anesthesia _____
11. Cystourethroscopy, steroid treatment of stricture _____
12. Suprapubic catheter aspiration of bladder _____
13. Exploratory nephrotomy _____
14. Partial excision of left kidney _____
15. Excision of Cowper's gland _____
16. Sling procedure for incontinence, 43-year-old male _____
17. Ureterolithotomy, stone in upper third _____
18. Plastic repair of ureter for stricture _____
19. Litholapaxy, 2.7 cm calculus _____
20. Marshall-Marchetti-Kranz procedure _____
21. Cystometrogram _____
22. Injection procedure for chain urethrocystography _____
23. Percutaneous placement of ureteral stent _____
24. Bilateral pyeloplasty for horseshoe kidney _____
25. Laser vaporization of prostate with TURP _____

Male Genital System

These codes identify procedures on the penis, testes, epididymis, tunica vaginalis, scrotum, vas deferens, spermatic cord, seminal vesicles, and prostate.

Watch for the worksheet item that has 2 possible answers.

Name _____

Male Genital System (54000–55899)

2012 CPT Codes

1. Newborn clamp circumcision _____
2. Traumatic partial amputation of penis _____
3. Punch biopsy of prostate _____
4. Bilateral hydrocelectomy _____
5. Radical retropubic prostatectomy _____
6. Urethroplasty, 3rd stage Cecil repair _____
7. Electroejaculation _____
8. Implantation of prosthetic testicle, left _____
9. Bilateral vasectomy _____
10. Chemical destruction of penile condyloma _____
11. Exploration of scrotum _____
12. Complex scrotoplasty _____
13. Insertion of radioactive pellet in prostate _____
14. One stage repair, perineal hypospadias with tube _____
15. Radical orchiectomy, abdominal exploration _____
16. Insertion of inflatable penile prosthesis _____
17. Abdominal vesiculectomy _____
18. Varicocelectomy with hernia repair _____
19. Abdominal exploration for undescended testis, bilateral _____
20. Plethysmography of penis _____
21. Biopsy and exploration of epididymis _____
22. Testicular biopsy via needle _____
23. Bilateral venous shunt for priapism _____
24. Complex prostatotomy for abscess _____
25. Vasovasorrhaphy _____

Intersex, Female Genital, and Maternity

This section defines reproductive system procedures; intersex surgery; procedures on the vulva, perineum and introitus, vagina, cervix and corpus uteri, oviducts, ovaries; and in vitro fertilization. Also included are the maternity services related to delivery, antepartum, and postpartum care.

There are several options for endoscopy in this section. You may need to read the procedure notes before coding the vulvar surgery as simple, radical, partial, or complete.

Note the services included in the prenatal or antepartum care. The instructions state: "other visits or services within this time period should be coded separately." This means that if you see a maternity patient for the flu or a burn, and you code it as unrelated to the pregnancy, you may bill it as an additional service. Would you bill inpatient medical care for the time your patient is hospitalized for delivery? No, not for the usual care associated with delivery, but you could report additional care for other complications. Also, another physician, following the patient for an unrelated difficulty, such as a cardiac problem, would bill for regular medical care as it is not related to the delivery.

Examine the instructions on partial prenatal care. Note that "abortion," not miscarriage, is the correct term for an uncompleted pregnancy. Abortions may be spontaneous, missed, septic, or induced.

Some worksheet items may require multiple codes or quantity indicators.

Name _____

Intersex, Female Genital, and Maternity (55920–59899)

2012 CPT Codes

1. Removal of 3 small leiomyomata by laparoscopy _____
2. Repair of rectovaginal fistula with colostomy _____
3. Intrauterine embryo transfer _____
4. Sex change surgery, female to male _____
5. Cervical LEEP biopsy, small electrode _____
6. Tubal occlusion with ring _____
7. Surgical treatment of second trimester missed abortion _____
8. Cystocele/urethrocele repair _____
9. Chorionic villus sampling by needle _____
10. Laparoscopic excision of pelvic lesions _____
11. Injection of dye for hysterosalpingogram _____
12. Salpingectomy for ectopic pregnancy, by laparoscopy _____
13. Vaginal delivery with tocolysis _____
14. Vaginal excision, 3 uterine fibroids, 240 grams _____
15. Cervical stump excision, repair of pelvic floor _____
16. Vaginal hysterectomy, partial vaginectomy, enterocele repair _____
17. Vaginal trachelorrhaphy _____
18. Laser destruction of extensive vaginal lesions _____
19. Complete pelvic exenteration _____
20. Bilateral excision of ovarian cysts _____
21. C-section delivery with postpartum care _____
22. Tubal ligation, 1 day after delivery _____
23. Fascial sling for stress incontinence _____
24. Biopsy perineum, 2 lesions _____
25. Hysteroscopy, lysis of adhesions _____

Endocrine and Nervous Systems

Procedures on the thyroid, parathyroid, thymus, and adrenal glands; carotid body; skull, meninges and brain; spine and spinal cord; extracranial and peripheral nerves; and autonomic nervous system, as well as destruction by neurolytic agent, neuroplasty, and neurorrhaphy are included on this worksheet.

The nervous system surgery is categorized by approach, definitive surgery, and reconstruction services and may be performed by more than one surgeon. You may want to refer to an anatomy text for clarification of the complex neurosurgical procedures.

Caution: Worksheet items 6 and 23. Don't forget modifiers and quantity where needed.

Name _____

Endocrine and Nervous Systems (60000–64999)

2012 CPT Codes

1. Subtotal thyroidectomy with radical neck dissection _____
2. Transcranial orbital exploration, removal of bullet _____
3. Intra-abdominal avulsion, vagus nerve _____
4. Laminectomy and excision of intradural sacral lesion _____
5. Single nerve graft, left arm, 4.5 cm _____
6. Injection procedure, lumbar Discogram (L4-L5) _____
7. Decompressive resection, single cervical vertebral body _____
8. Remove and replace CSF shunt system _____
9. Percutaneous stereotactic chemical lesion, trigeminal _____
10. Excision of thyroid adenoma _____
11. Paracervical nerve block for delivery _____
12. Repeat subdural tap through suture, newborn _____
13. Excision with graft of infected intradural bone _____
14. Total removal of implanted spinal neurostimulator receiver _____
15. Bone flap craniotomy for cerebellopontine tumor _____
16. Suture thenar motor nerve, right hand _____
17. Exploratory burr hole, supratentorial, bilateral _____
18. Repair complex dural intracranial AV malformation _____
19. Cervical hemilaminectomy/re-exploration and decompression _____
20. Brain stem biopsy, transoral/split mandible approach _____
21. Excision of carotid body tumor and artery _____
22. Craniectomy for posterior fossa tumor _____
23. Cable nerve grafts, 3 cm left arm and 4.5 cm left leg _____
24. LeFort osteotomy with fixation, anterior fossa _____
25. Cranioplasty for 6.5 cm skull defect _____

Eye and Ocular Adnexa

This section lists procedures on the eyeballs, cornea, iris, ciliary body, lens, vitreous, retina, eye muscles, bony orbit, eyelids, conjunctiva, and lacrimal system.

Note the distinction between ocular and orbital implants. There are many laser procedures for the eye. Removal of a cataract may include other services. The surgeon may do the lens implant as a single stage procedure at the time the cataract is removed, or later.

Since there are two eyes and two ears, the -RT and -LT modifiers are especially important in the next two sections.

Watch for add-on or multiple codes and modifiers.

Name _____

Eye and Ocular Adnexa (65091–68899)

2012 CPT Codes

1. Probe/irrigate left nasolacrimal duct under general _____
2. One laser treatment session, 3 small retinal breaks, left _____
3. Exploration left orbit, remove embedded nailhead _____
4. Excise 0.75 cm conjunctival lesion, left eye _____
5. Reinsert ocular implant with conjunctival graft, right _____
6. Revise operative site, right anterior segment _____
7. Removal of posterior FB with magnet, left eye _____
8. Left tarsal wedge excision for ectropion _____
9. Peripheral iridectomy for glaucoma, left _____
10. Correction of right surgical astigmatism by wedge _____
11. External levator repair, right blepharoptosis _____
12. Enucleation, insertion of muscle-stabilized implant, left _____
13. Repeat scleral buckling, old retinal detachment, left _____
14. Excise lower lid chalazions, 3 left, 1 right _____
15. Right corneal laceration repair with tissue glue _____
16. Laser treatment of left vitreous strands _____
17. Removal of right dacryolith _____
18. Laser trabeculoplasty, right _____
19. Discission of left secondary cataract by incision _____
20. Total reconstruction, right upper lid _____
21. Extracapsular phacoemulsification with lens implant, left _____
22. Posterior fixation for strabismus, resect 2 horizontal muscles, right eye _____
23. Single plug closure, right lacrimal punctum _____
24. Bilateral antibiotic injection, anterior chamber _____
25. Initial superior oblique strabismus surgery, left _____

Auditory System

This section includes procedures on the external, middle, and inner ear, and the temporal bone. After the eye, coding the ear services seems easy.

Caution: One worksheet item needs an add-on code; most need modifiers.

Auditory System (69000–69990)

2012 CPT Codes

1. Replace left temporal bone conduction device
2. Bilateral otoplasty for severely protruding ears
3. Total facial nerve suture and graft, with operating microscope
4. Repeat right mastoidectomy, now radical
5. Excision of right external ear cyst
6. Neurectomy, right tympanic membrane
7. Postauricular middle ear exploration, left
8. Simple mastoidectomy, right
9. Semicircular canal fenestration, left
10. Stapedotomy, repair of right ossicular chain
11. Catheterize/inflate left eustachian tube, transnasal
12. Right oval window fistula repair
13. Facial nerve repair, medial/geniculate, left
14. Left tube tympanostomy with Novocaine
15. Subtotal amputation, right external ear
16. Cochlear implant, right
17. Excision polyp, left ear
18. Remove FB left external ear, general anesthesia
19. I&D of abscess, left external meatus
20. Myringoplasty, right
21. Left mastoidectomy with labyrinthectomy
22. Excision of neoplasm, left temporal bone
23. Mastoidectomy/tympanoplasty, reconstruct right ossicular chain
24. Excision left extratemporal glomus tumor
25. Routine cleaning of right mastoid cavity

Radiology

The first worksheet of radiographic procedures covers the section on diagnostic radiology and imaging. It includes flat films of the head and neck, chest, spine, pelvis, and upper and lower extremities. These studies are the most common radiologic procedures performed in the physician's office.

The second worksheet includes studies of the abdomen, gastrointestinal and urinary tracts, and gynecological and obstetrical services. It also includes diagnostic imaging of the heart, aorta and arteries, and veins and lymphatics. It concludes with transcatheter procedures, transluminal atherectomy, and other therapeutic procedures.

The third worksheet covers three sections. The first section, diagnostic ultrasound or "echo," includes procedures for diagnosis and guidance. The second section, radiation oncology, provides codes for clinical treatment planning, delivery and management, hyperthermia, and brachytherapy. The last section, diagnostic nuclear medicine, has codes for the endocrine, lymphatic, gastrointestinal, musculoskeletal, cardiovascular, respiratory, nervous, and genitourinary systems, and therapeutic nuclear studies.

Radiology services, the 70,000 codes, are one of the non-surgical sections in CPT. This section has special instructions, unlisted procedure codes, and modifiers. The "supervision and interpretation" services correspond to many of the injection procedures in previous surgical sections. Many of the "S&I" codes are followed by a reference to the surgical part of the diagnostic service. The Interventional Radiology Coding Users' Guide is very helpful in explaining these services.

Many specialists perform S&I studies, not just radiologists. Note that a written report, signed by the doctor interpreting the study, is part of the service and may not be billed separately. Nuclear medicine, once limited to the hospital setting, is now part of some medical practices.

Remember that the service at the doctor's office is the global or complete service, both the professional and technical components. The same study performed at the hospital must be reported as the "professional component," as the doctor does not own the equipment. The facility reports the "technical component" to be paid for the equipment, staff, supplies, lights, and other expenses associated with the service. With very few exceptions, when the place of service is 21 (inpatient), 22 (outpatient), or 23 (emergency department), the 7xxxx service will require the modifier –26.

Move slowly through this section, reading all instructions and definitions. If you are confused by words ending in "gram" or "graphy," think of telegram and telegraphy. One is the result, the other the process.

Watch for items requiring modifiers or multiple codes.

Radiology – I (70010–73725)

2012 CPT Codes

1. S&I arthrography, left knee
2. Four views, nasal fracture
3. X-ray of right knee, 4 views
4. CT of pelvis, with contrast
5. Neck CT with and without contrast and additional sections
6. Pelvis, 2 views
7. X-ray left eye, no foreign body
8. Scoliosis x-ray study of the spine
9. Chest x-ray, 1 view
10. TMJ arthrography, supervision/interpretation
11. Physician-administered functional MRI
12. Two views right 4th finger
13. Cervical MRI, no contrast
14. X-ray teeth, right upper, left upper and lower
15. Two views cervical spine, outpatient
16. Right leg x-ray, 2-month-old baby boy
17. Bilateral fractured ribs, 3 views
18. X-ray elbow, PA and Lateral
19. Complete study left hip
20. Neck MRI, no contrast, inpatient
21. X-ray exam left scapula, 3 views
22. CT thoracic spine with contrast
23. Proton imaging for lymph nodes, chest
24. X-ray right sialolith
25. Cervical myelogram S&I

Name _____

Radiology – II (74000–76499)

2012 CPT Codes

1. Upper GI exam with delayed films and KUB _____
2. Bilateral selective adrenal venography, S&I _____
3. Videography of swallowing _____
4. Acute abdomen series _____
5. Cineradiography in operating room _____
6. Bilateral selective adrenal angiography, S&I _____
7. Supervise/interpret voiding urethrocystography _____
8. Bilateral femoral intravascular ultrasound _____
9. S&I, transcatheter removal of broken catheter _____
10. LeVeen shuntogram, S&I _____
11. Barium enema, KUB study _____
12. Contrast monitoring to change percutaneous drain tube, S&I _____
13. S&I, bilateral carotid neck angiogram _____
14. Retrograde urography with KUB _____
15. Percutaneous transhepatic portography, S&I, in ER _____
16. S&I, hysterosalpingogram _____
17. Supervise/interpret AV shunt angiogram _____
18. Fluoroscopy, 50 minutes by non-GI physician _____
19. Thoracic aortography by serialography, S&I _____
20. Perineogram _____
21. Lymphangiography, right arm, S&I _____
22. Consult/report on x-rays done at University Hospital _____
23. Transhepatic percutaneous cholangiography, S&I _____
24. Follow-up CT study, localized _____
25. Cardiac MRI and stress imaging, with and without contrast _____

Name _____

Radiology – III (76506–79999)

2012 CPT Codes

1. Complete obstetrical B-scan, 18 weeks, twin pregnancy _____
2. Thyroid, metastatic CA imaging, total body _____
3. Simulation treatment planning, right hip and knee _____
4. SPECT cardiac rest and exercise studies at hospital _____
5. Lymph gland imaging _____
6. Voiding cystogram reflux study with residual bladder study _____
7. Radiation treatment: Left shoulder and hip, 7.5 MeV _____
8. Pulmonary ventilation and perfusion study _____
9. Transrectal echo _____
10. Intracavitary element placement, 11 ribbons, outpatient _____
11. Combined B-12 absorption study _____
12. Radioelement placement, surface of left forearm _____
13. Ophthalmic biometry A-scan _____
14. External hyperthermia, 2.7 cm deep _____
15. Splenic red cell survival measurement _____
16. First pass cardiac resting study _____
17. Brachytherapy planning, 2 sources _____
18. SPECT bone imaging, professional component only _____
19. Radiopharmaceutical treatment via joint infusion _____
20. Ultrasound guidance for needle biopsy, S&I _____
21. Radiopharmaceutical localization, lung abscess _____
22. Neutron radiation, 1 area _____
23. Repeat fetal Doppler echocardiogram _____
24. Ultrasound guidance for amniocentesis, S&I _____
25. SPECT liver imaging _____

Pathology and Laboratory

Lab worksheet Part I covers lab panels, drug testing, therapeutic drug assays, evocative/suppression testing, clinical pathology consultations, urinalysis, and ends with chemistry tests. Note that the chemistry tests are listed in alphabetic order.

Part II includes molecular diagnostics, hematology, coagulation, immunology, and tissue typing.

The final lab worksheet describes transfusion medicine, microbiology, anatomic pathology, including postmortem examination and cytopathology, cytogenics, surgical pathology, and miscellaneous laboratory services, ending with reproductive medicine procedures.

Reimbursement varies widely for laboratory studies. Review the manuals for the office testing equipment to determine the correct code for each study. Do not take the word of the equipment salesperson.

A federal regulation, the Clinical Laboratory Improvement Act (CLIA), rated laboratory tests by complexity. Each lab is certified to perform a specified level of testing. Some physicians discontinued all office laboratory work. Other practices reduced their laboratory work to only basic, uncomplicated services.

As you complete the worksheets, review the guidelines and look for instructions within each subsection. A few codes include the physician's services. Watch for the lab tests with legal implications. Unlike the surgical services, the clinical laboratory tests may be numbered so that the lowest code number identifies the most comprehensive study. A few describe testing you can do safely at home.

Some worksheet items require multiple codes or quantity reporting.

Name _____

Pathology and Laboratory – I (80047–83887)

2012 CPT Codes

1. Four studies each, luteinizing hormone and FSH _____
2. Quantitative theophylline screen, blood _____
3. Occult blood in stool, 3 guaiac test cards for neoplasm screen _____
4. Qualitative cystine/homocystine, urine _____
5. Urinary amino acids, quantitative, 3 specimens _____
6. Glucose tolerance test, 4 specimens _____
7. Blood ethanol levels _____
8. Full sequence analysis BRCA1 and 2 _____
9. Atomic spectroscopy, manganese _____
10. HDL cholesterol direct measurement _____
11. Manual microscopic urinalysis _____
12. Blood catecholamines _____
13. Creatinine clearance _____
14. Obstetric panel of tests _____
15. Hemoglobin, methemoglobin, qualitative _____
16. Folic acid RBC _____
17. Cocaine drug screening _____
18. Estriol _____
19. Color pregnancy test, urine _____
20. Total serum cholesterol _____
21. Hepatitis A,B,C antibodies, B surface antigens _____
22. Fractionation (17-KS) ketosteroids _____
23. CRH stimulation panel _____
24. Mucopolysaccharide screen _____
25. TSH panel, 4 studies, 2 hours _____

Name _____

Pathology and Laboratory – II (83890–86849)

2012 CPT Codes

1. Total blood protein, Western Blot _____
2. Quantitative D-dimer degraded fibrin _____
3. PKU blood test, 2-day-old infant _____
4. Routine prothrombin time _____
5. Vitamin E _____
6. Total T cell with absolute CD4 and 8 _____
7. Single nucleic acid probe _____
8. Eastern equine encephalitis antibody test _____
9. Clotting factor VIII, single stage _____
10. Vitamin B-2 _____
11. C-reactive protein _____
12. Parathyroid hormone _____
13. Heparin neutralization _____
14. HLA typing, A, single antigen _____
15. Strip test, urea nitrogen _____
16. Skin test for histoplasmosis _____
17. Chorionic gonadotropin, qualitative _____
18. Hepatitis C antibody _____
19. Total testosterone _____
20. Platelet antibody identification _____
21. Urinary potassium _____
22. Total clotting inhibitor, protein S _____
23. Blood/urine Xylose absorption test _____
24. Rubella antibody screen _____
25. Double-strand DNA antibody _____

Name _____

Pathology and Laboratory – III (86850–89398)

2012 CPT Codes

1. Platelet pooling _____
2. Bone marrow tissue analysis for malignancy _____
3. Scanning electron microscopy _____
4. Stool culture for salmonella _____
5. Coroner-ordered autopsy _____
6. Surgical pathology, gross/micro, uterus with tumor _____
7. Flow cytometry, DNA analysis _____
8. Rabbit inoculation, observation _____
9. Influenza detection by immunoassay _____
10. Gross autopsy, including brain _____
11. Surgical pathology, gross/micro cholesteatoma _____
12. Preoperative autologous blood collection/storage _____
13. Motility, volume and count semen analysis _____
14. Consult/report on slides from University Hospital _____
15. Antibiotic sensitivity study, 10 disks _____
16. Chlamydia culture _____
17. Limited chromosome analysis/banding, amniotic fluid _____
18. KOH skin slide prep _____
19. Forensic cytopathology for sperm _____
20. CSF cell count with differential _____
21. Thawing fresh frozen plasma, 2 units _____
22. Immunofluorescent detection Type 1 Herpes _____
23. Preparations for nerve teasing _____
24. Collection of vaginal smear for dark field exam _____
25. Intraoperative consultation and frozen section, 2 specimens _____

Medicine

Worksheet I covers injections, psychiatry, dialysis services, diagnostic medical services for gastroenterology, and non-surgical procedures on the eye and ear.

The second worksheet has cardiovascular and pulmonary diagnostic and therapeutic services, procedures for allergy, and neurology.

Worksheet III includes chemotherapy and physical medicine. The special services of osteopaths and chiropractors, additional anesthesia codes, and other special procedures and services are the final subsections of CPT. The Category II and III codes may not be accepted by all insurance plans. Some of the special services, procedures, and reports also may be excluded from payment.

Many CPTs ago, office visits were part of the Medicine section. Then they became evaluation and management services and are now listed separately. The invasive procedures in this section are diagnostic and are usually considered non-surgical. This may seem strange since coronary angioplasty, the procedure some people have instead of open-heart surgery, is in this section.

Many doctors use services from this section, such as injections, EKGs, and pulmonary function testing. Generally, as you can see from the subsection listing, these services belong to a medical specialty. Study these services carefully. The guidelines for this section are familiar. Now we apply them to medical procedures rather than surgery.

Caution: Watch for multiple codes, modifiers, and quantity reporting.

Name _____

Medicine – I (90281–92700)

2012 CPT Codes

1. Endothelial microscopy, cell count, photo/report _____
2. Medical hypnotherapy to stop smoking _____
3. One mini IM dose Rho(d) _____
4. Tinnitus assessment, right ear _____
5. Rhinomanometry _____
6. Binaural hearing aid exam _____
7. Manometric studies, anus and rectum _____
8. Bernstein test for esophagitis _____
9. Tangent screen visual fields, right eye _____
10. Supply Tetanus vaccine for use with jet injector, 27-year-old male _____
11. Hepatitis B immunization series, first visit, 19-year-old dialysis patient _____
12. Biofeedback training for arrhythmia _____
13. Monthly dialysis monitoring, 16-year-old female, 1 visit _____
14. Insight-oriented psychotherapy, 1 hour and 15 minutes, in the office _____
15. Psychotherapy with family, patient absent _____
16. Comprehensive eye exam, new patient _____
17. Fluorescein multiframe angiography, complete _____
18. Contact lens replacement, right _____
19. Impedance tympanometry _____
20. Dialysis training, one session _____
21. Air audiometry _____
22. Fitting of bifocal lenses _____
23. Multiple seizure electroconvulsive treatments, one session _____
24. Audiometry by select picture _____
25. Inpatient non-verbal psychotherapy with medical visit, 45 minutes _____

Name _____

Medicine – II (92950–96020)

2012 CPT Codes

1. Coronary thrombolysis by IV infusion _____
2. Inpatient right and left heart cath, congenital heart defect _____
3. Interp/report only, tilt table cardiac testing _____
4. Pulmonary percutaneous balloon valvuloplasty _____
5. EMG cranial nerve supplied muscles, bilateral _____
6. Dispense 15 doses antigen, bee and wasp _____
7. Brief study, transcranial Doppler _____
8. Cardiac stress test, tracing only _____
9. Awake/sleep EEG, 10 p.m. to 7 a.m. _____
10. CPAP _____
11. Scratch tests, 10 trees, 3 venom _____
12. Electromyography, 10 muscles, while running on treadmill _____
13. Twenty-four-hour ECG, recording only _____
14. Complete service, 1 month patient-activated spirometry recording _____
15. Repeat analysis of cranial nerve stimulator implant _____
16. Myasthenia gravis challenge test _____
17. His Bundle recording _____
18. Complete 4 extremity plethysmography _____
19. Venous Doppler, both legs, complete study _____
20. Transesophageal echocardiogram, total service _____
21. Ear oximetry for O_2 saturation _____
22. S&I for ventricular angiography during left heart cath _____
23. Stress echocardiogram, complete _____
24. Complete ambulatory blood pressure monitoring, 32 hours _____
25. Electrical testing of blink reflex _____

Name _____

Medicine – III (96040–0290T)

2012 CPT Codes

1. Nurse visit to patient's home for urinary catheter change _____
2. Poisoning treatment with Ipecac, observation _____
3. Iontophoresis, 35 minutes _____
4. Limited developmental testing with report _____
5. OMT, head and neck _____
6. IV conscious sedation, 25 minutes, 67-year-old male, for esophageal dilation _____
7. Phone evaluation, 25 minutes with suicidal patient who just returned from 2 months in Europe _____
8. Acupuncture, 4 needles _____
9. Documented assessment for risk of falls _____
10. Breath test for rejection of heart transplant _____
11. Telogen/antigen counts on hair clipped at the lab _____
12. Psychiatric screening to determine suicide risk _____
13. Behavior intervention, 30 minutes, twins and both parents _____
14. Three hours medical testimony _____
15. Initial nurse visit for infant born at home _____
16. Scalpel wound debridement, 14.5 sq cm _____
17. Reevaluation of physical therapy treatment _____
18. Diabetic meal planning education, 1 hour, 4 patients _____
19. Home visit and enema for fecal impaction _____
20. Patient education/counseling, prescribed beta-blocker medication _____
21. Chemotherapy, arterial infusion, 55 minutes _____
22. Gait and stairs retraining, 30 minutes _____
23. IM chemotherapy administration _____
24. Chiropractic treatment, 2 spinal areas _____
25. Home visit infusion, 5-year-old female with hemophilia, 1.5 hours _____

HCPCS LEVEL II CODES

Developed by the federal government, HCPCS (Healthcare Common Procedure Coding System) National Level II codes identify over 5,000 codes and descriptive terminology for services not included in CPT. HCPCS provides codes for reporting supplies, injectables, and the services of non-physician providers such as ambulance companies and Medicaid programs. HCPCS code changes start on January 1 with CPT.

Level II HCPCS codes begin with a letter followed by 4 digits. Although the codes were originally designed for Medicare and Medicaid, they are part of the HIPAA designated code sets and most private insurers accept and understand them. Medicare, Medicaid, and some other payers may require the provider to register as a Durable Medical Equipment (DME) supplier before payment can be made for some supplies and equipment.

HCPCS lists codes alphabetically. Some Level II sections are unusual. D (dental) codes were eliminated in 2012 at the request of the American Dental Association. K codes are used only by Durable Medical Equipment Medicare Administrative Contractors (DME MACs) and are temporary codes. Many M (medical) services eventually appear in CPT so this list changes each year. Q codes are temporary codes, sometimes appearing mid-year when it becomes necessary to identify a service previously included in or reported by another code. Medicare and Medicaid bulletins will tell you when to report a new Q code. S codes may be used by the Blues, Medicaid, and Commercial payers to facilitate claims processing and are not valid for the Medicare program. Medicaid programs asked for the inclusion of the T codes that may also be used by private insurers, but never for Medicare.

Read the introduction for an explanation of the HCPCS reference. Each of the sections begins with guidelines on how to use the codes correctly. There may be a mini-index to that section. The HCPCS index may show a single code, a range of codes, or provide no listing for that service. Like the CPT index, you may need to think of other ways to describe the service if you are to find the correct code.

HCPCS modifiers appear in the Appendix or near the front of the book. Another Appendix contains a summary of code changes. A different appendix has a list of modified or deleted codes. There are two sorted lists in HCPCS, a table of drugs and a general index. Many private companies print versions of this codebook. Your reference may have numbers or letters to identify each appendix, or differ in format, but the codes and descriptions should be consistent with all vendors. These companies may provide an expanded index or additional information on the use of these codes.

As you code the worksheet, start with the index. Then verify the code(s) with the actual code section, as there may be sizes, quantities, or other variables in selecting the correct code. Read the guidelines to be certain you select the proper code. Many terms are similar and may be unfamiliar. If you use these codes in your work, consult with your employer to be certain you report the correct code.

HCPCS has special alphanumeric or two-letter modifiers. Some of these are included in the Modifier worksheet.

Name _____

HCPCS Level II Codes

2012 HCPCS

1. Delivery of monaural behind-the-ear hearing aid _____
2. Medicaid case management, 1 month _____
3. Injection, 100,000 units of Bicillin CR _____
4. Premolded removable metatarsal support, right foot _____
5. Chelation therapy _____
6. Wellness assessment by a nurse practitioner _____
7. Right shoe modified with outside sole wedge _____
8. Dispensed 60 days of prenatal vitamins _____
9. Injection, 8 mg Compazine _____
10. Preschool screening for language problems _____
11. Vinyl urinary bag with tube and leg strap _____
12. Custom made plastic artificial eye _____
13. Obtained Pap smear, sent to lab _____
14. Methotrexate, 50 mg _____
15. Non-emergency transportation by wheelchair van _____
16. Nasogastric tubing, no stylet _____
17. Adjustable aluminum three-prong cane, with tips _____
18. Non-sterile dialysis gloves, 1 box of 100 _____
19. Mitomycin, 5 mg _____
20. Took x-ray to nursing home, 1 patient seen _____
21. Hook hand prosthesis, closing _____
22. Injection, Estradiol, 9 mg _____
23. Needleless injection device _____
24. Toronto orthosis for Legg Perthes _____
25. Recording apnea monitor, high-risk infant _____

Modifiers

Modifiers are two-character suffixes for procedure codes. They provide important information on how that service changed in some way without altering the definition of the code. Using modifiers properly eliminates some of the need to send procedure notes with claims. All CPT modifiers are two-digit numbers and HCPCS modifiers are two letters or a letter and digit. Some modifiers apply to evaluation and management services only while others clarify surgical procedures. Both CPT and HCPCS provide a complete list of modifiers in an appendix.

CPT modifiers may indicate a reduced or expanded service, bilateral procedures, or the professional component of a service. HCPCS modifiers may indicate the rental or purchase of a piece of equipment, services by a social worker, or that the services were provided in a medically underserved area. Medicare and Medicaid may also direct you to apply HCPCS modifiers to CPT codes. Like the codes they modify, modifiers may be changed or eliminated with each new edition of CPT and HCPCS.

Modifiers may be shown as –22 or –AN. The "–" is not reported but is useful if you write out a code as "12345–22" or "54321–LT." The claim form and computer files have special columns or fields for modifiers. Some payers may ask you to report modifiers as a five-character code, 09922 or 099LT.

The worksheet requires a modifier for each scenario. Use the appendix in the CPT and HCPCS codebooks to select the correct two-character modifier. Some items may require multiple answers.

Name _____

Modifiers

2012 CPT

1. The patient had major surgery by Dr. Jones on July 16, and saw the doctor on August 4 for an unrelated office visit. The August 4 service requires modifier: _____

2. Dr. Brown asks Dr. White to assist in a major surgery because a surgery resident is not available. Dr. White reports the surgery code with modifier: _____

3. When an insurer requires a presurgical second opinion, the service is reported with the modifier: _____

4. The surgery was difficult because the patient was a paraplegic weighing 427 pounds. To report these circumstances to the insurer, use modifier: _____

5. Dr. Gray, the family doctor, asks a surgeon, Dr. Green, to see Mrs. Brown at City Hospital, as she may need surgery. Dr. Green schedules the surgery for tomorrow and reports today's service with modifier: _____

6. Dr. Thomas does an appendectomy and removes a mole from the patient's neck while in the OR. Use modifier ___ on the ___ service line of the claim form. _____

2012 HCPCS

7. Dr. Reed, a clinical psychologist, saw a Medicare patient for diagnostic testing. Dr. Reed reports 96101 with modifier: _____

8. If you refile a claim and change the procedure code because it was incorrect on the original claim, use modifier: _____

9. When a procedure is recorded on an analog tape recorder, use modifier QT. For a digital recording, use: _____

10. Dr. Johns owns the portable x-ray equipment, but Dr. Hopkins does the interpretation and report. Identify the modifiers for both doctors: _____

11. Dr. Little sees patients in an inner city clinic, designated as physician scarcity area. He receives additional compensation for these services by reporting modifier: _____

12. Mr. Small obtains a cane from the medical supply store. If it was a new cane, report modifier: _____

INTRODUCTION TO IDC-9-CM

Diagnosis coding systems are older than procedure coding methods. More than 100 years ago a French physician developed a system for coding causes of death. In the early 1900s, the U.S. Public Health Service (PHS) began using the same codes. The World Health Organization (WHO) developed ICD-8 in the late 1930s. In 1950, the PHS and the Veterans Administration (VA) adopted ICD-8, the International Classification of Disease, Eighth Revision, Adapted. With the U.S. implementation of ICDA-8 (ICD Adapted), our information on mortality and morbidity could be matched with statistics from the rest of the world.

Non-governmental hospitals began to use ICDA-8, and the PHS expanded the system to include codes for surgery and treatment. Private agencies were also developing coding structures and by the 1960s, the United States used at least two diagnosis coding systems. In 1979, the government mandated the use of a new system, ICD-9-CM, for reporting services to Medicare and Medicaid, later extended to all payers by HIPAA.

The ICD-9-CM, International Classification of Disease, Ninth Revision, Clinical Modification, is compatible with the WHO system, ICD-9. Congress required a standardized coding system for the implementation of Diagnosis Related Groups (DRGs), in 1983. The DRGs are Medicare's hospital payment method. All the diagnoses in ICD-9-CM are grouped into fewer than 500 DRGs. The hospital receives payment for the patient's DRG category, not the cost of the patient's care.

After the government standardized the diagnosis coding system, many private organizations started printing ICD-9-CM with improvements. Some place a color-coded box over the numbers that need a fourth or fifth digit; some distribute the codes in a ring binder; others have anatomical drawings throughout that illustrate the codes. You may buy a loose-leaf subscription for updated pages from some agencies. The government maintains the codes but no longer prints an annual edition of ICD-9-CM. They do warn that they are not responsible for the errors made by others in printing the codes.

ICD-9-CM updates codes quarterly but if the office buys a new book each August, it should be safe to use for the next year. The publishers usually print the year prominently on the cover so you know when the book becomes obsolete. If the office subscribes to an update service for a loose-leaf ICD-9-CM, remember the October 1st implementation date, as you may not notice if you fail to receive the new pages.

The doctor's office uses two of the three volumes of ICD-9-CM. Volume 1, the Tabular List, provides the codes by body system, in numeric order. Volume 2, the Alphabetic Index, contains many diagnoses that are missing in the Tabular List. After finding the diagnosis in Alphabetic Index, it must be verified with Tabular List. If you use only the Alphabetic Index or only the Tabular List you may select an incorrect code. For convenience, the books are frequently printed with the alphabetical index first. Volume 3 of ICD-9-CM contains procedure codes used by hospitals. The doctor's office uses CPT for reporting services, not Volume 3.

Many physicians' offices use only 50 to 100 diagnosis codes. Rather than look them up each time, codes appear on encounter forms or "cheat sheets" used by the billers. There are two problems with this approach. First, the list restricts the number of diagnoses available. Do all the patients have only two or three kinds of hypertension? Second, the office must update the codes on an annual basis. Maybe they review these codes only when they need to order encounter forms. Unfortunately, if you order forms in August, your forms may not have the updated codes required for the next year.

It seems reasonable to assume that with all the updating of codes, we will eventually need a completely new system. ICD-10-CM will be enacted officially on October 1, 2013. Other HIPAA mandated changes must be implemented first. Until then, you must become familiar with ICD-9-CM. The worksheets contain columns for both ICD-9-CM and for ICD-10-CM, if you have access to a draft of the new manual.

Using ICD-9-CM

The office may code either the principal diagnosis or the primary diagnosis for the patient visit. The principal diagnosis is the condition found after study. The primary diagnosis is the reason for the visit. Suppose you see a patient complaining of abdominal pain. If you can establish the cause, such as acute appendicitis, you may report that code. If the complaints are vague, maybe the flu, the threat of layoffs at work, or an upcoming week of final exams, the doctor may code "abdominal pain" for the office visit. Hospitals use the principal diagnosis.

While using CPT, we find very few services described by a person's name, an eponym. A medical term or anatomical description identified most procedures. One exception to this rule is bunion surgery where proper names are used to differentiate surgical techniques, such as Mitchell, Keller, McBride, etc. Diagnoses frequently use a person's name: Parkinson's or Cushing's disease, or a Bennett fracture. This is probably because the diagnosis coding system is older and diseases were traditionally named for the physician first reporting the condition.

As you do with CPT, you will need to become familiar with the diagnosis-coding conventions. The medical office should observe the rules on "includes" and "excludes" but we may have limited use for the "code also underlying disease" if it is not specified in the medical record. Before beginning the worksheets, take time to review the introduction, the terminology, and the format of the Tabular and Alphabetic volumes. Some editions of ICD-9-CM are specifically designed for coding in the doctor's office. If you are fortunate enough to have one of those, read all the preliminary information for many helpful hints on using ICD-9-CM.

Diagnosis Coding - Quick and Dirty

Billers receive many invitations to attend seminars on the fine art of diagnosis coding. The instructors are frequently medical records people who must be exact in their hospital reporting. They emphasize accuracy above all else. Unfortunately, it is not that easy in the doctor's office. The diagnosis coding system was developed to collect information worldwide on the presence of disease. We must use the same system to defend charging for medical services. As an example, there are few problems not made worse by obesity. Since obesity is not the problem we are treating, it is not mentioned. If fact, many insurers would not pay for any service billed with the diagnosis of obesity.

Mental health and other programs may authorize a limited number of services and specify the diagnosis code to use for those visits. To be paid, you must report the authorized diagnosis even if the visit concerned other problems.

Also, the doctor's office may be limited to a few diagnoses per service. We simply must list first the "best" diagnosis code for the service. Diagnosis codes must be reasonable for the service performed. Always subject your coding to a reasonableness test. The next worksheet will show you how. The answers appear after The Ten Commandments of Diagnosis Coding. Section IV of the ICD-9-CM Official Guidelines for Coding and Reporting appear after Reasonableness Testing.

Reasonableness Testing

Procedures and diagnoses must be reasonable; they must match each other. No one will declare it reasonable to x-ray a foot for a broken wrist. To assure that your choices come from the correct sections, the summary tables are presented below.

Diagnoses
1. 001-139   Infectious/Parasitic Disease
2. 140-239   Neoplasms
3. 240-279   Endocrine/Nutrition/Immunity
4. 280-289   Blood/Blood-Forming Organs
5. 290-319   Mental Disorders
6. 320-389   Nervous System/Sense Organs
7. 390-459   Circulatory Systems
8. 460-519   Respiratory System
9. 520-579   Digestive System
10. 580-629   Genitourinary System
11. 630-679   Pregnancy/Childbirth
12. 680-709   Skin/Subcutaneous Tissue
13. 710-739   Musculoskeletal/Connective Tissue
14. 740-759   Congenital Anomalies
15. 760-779   Perinatal Conditions
16. 780-799   Symptoms/Signs/Ill-Defined Conditions
17. 800-999   Injury/Poisoning
18. V01-V91   Health Status/Contact V-codes
19. E800-E999   External Causes E-codes

Procedures
1. 99201-99499   Evaluation/Management
2. 00100-01999   Anesthesia
3. 10021-19499   Integumentary System
4. 20000-29999   Musculoskeletal System
5. 30000-32999   Respiratory System
6. 33010-37799   Cardiovascular System
7. 38100-39599   Hemic/Lymph/Mediastinum
8. 40490-49999   Digestive System
9. 50010-53899   Urinary System
10. 54000-55899   Male Genital System
11. 55970-59899   Intersex/Female/Maternity
12. 60000-64999   Endocrine/Nervous Systems
13. 65091-68899   Eye/Ocular Adnexa
14. 69000-69990   Auditory System
15. 70010-79999   Radiology Services
16. 80047-89398   Pathology Services
17. 90281-99607   Medical Services
18. 0001F-0290T   Category II and III Codes

Using these tables, we can determine "reasonable" coding sections for procedures and diagnoses. If we assume there are no significant complications, we can select the reasonable code ranges for a fractured finger:

Diagnoses: Musculoskeletal (13), Injury (17), External Causes (19)
Procedures: E/M (1), Musculoskeletal (3), Radiology (15)

Using the code section numbers, identify diagnoses and procedures for:

1. Headache: Diagnoses:
                     Procedures:
2. Pneumothorax: Diagnoses:
                     Procedures:
3. Ulcer: Diagnoses:
                     Procedures:

ICD-9-CM Official Guidelines for Coding and Reporting

Section IV. Diagnostic Coding and Reporting Guidelines for Outpatient Services

These coding guidelines for outpatient diagnoses have been approved for use by hospitals/providers in coding and reporting hospital-based outpatient services and provider-based office visits.

Information about the use of certain abbreviations, punctuation, symbols, and other conventions used in the ICD-9-CM Tabular List (code numbers and titles), can be found in Section IA of these guidelines, under "Conventions Used in the Tabular List." Information about the correct sequence to use in finding a code is also described in Section I.

The terms encounter and visit are often used interchangeably in describing outpatient service contacts and, therefore, appear together in these guidelines without distinguishing one from the other.

Though the conventions and general guidelines apply to all settings, coding guidelines for outpatient and provider reporting of diagnoses will vary in a number of instances from those for inpatient diagnoses, recognizing that:

> The Uniform Hospital Discharge Data Set (UHDDS) definition of principal diagnosis applies only to inpatients in acute, short-term, long-term care and psychiatric hospitals.
>
> Coding guidelines for inconclusive diagnoses (probable, suspected, rule out, etc.) were developed for inpatient reporting and do not apply to outpatients.

A. Selection of first-listed condition

> In the outpatient setting, the term first-listed diagnosis is used in lieu of principal diagnosis.

In determining the first-listed diagnosis the coding conventions of ICD-9-CM, as well as the general and disease specific guidelines take precedence over the outpatient guidelines.

Diagnoses often are not established at the time of the initial encounter/visit. It may take two or more visits before the diagnosis is confirmed.

The most critical rule involves beginning the search for the correct code assignment through the Alphabetic Index. Never begin searching initially in the Tabular List as this will lead to coding errors.

1. Outpatient Surgery

When a patient presents for outpatient surgery, code the reason for the surgery as the first-listed diagnosis (reason for the encounter), even if the surgery is not performed due to a contraindication.

2. Observation Stay

When a patient is admitted for observation for a medical condition, assign a code for the medical condition as the first-listed diagnosis.

When a patient presents for outpatient surgery and develops complications requiring admission to observation, code the reason for the surgery as the first reported diagnosis (reason for the encounter), followed by codes for the complications as secondary diagnoses.

B. Codes from 001.0 through V91.99

The appropriate code or codes from 001.0 through V91.99 must be used to identify diagnoses, symptoms, conditions, problems, complaints, or other reason(s) for the encounter/visit.

C. Accurate reporting of ICD-9-CM diagnosis codes

For accurate reporting of ICD-9-CM diagnosis codes, the documentation should describe the patient's condition, using terminology which includes specific diagnoses as well as symptoms, problems, or reasons for the encounter. There are ICD-9-CM codes to describe all of these.

D. Selection of codes 001.0 through 999.9

The selection of codes 001.0 through 999.9 will frequently be used to describe the reason for the encounter. These codes are from the section of ICD-9-CM for the classification of diseases and injuries (e.g. infectious and parasitic diseases; neoplasms; symptoms, signs, and ill-defined conditions, etc.).

E. Codes that describe symptoms and signs

Codes that describe symptoms and signs, as opposed to diagnoses, are acceptable for reporting purposes when a diagnosis has not been established (confirmed) by the provider. Chapter 16 of ICD-9-CM, Symptoms, Signs, and Ill-defined conditions (codes 780.0 - 799.9) contain many, but not all codes for symptoms.

F. Encounters for circumstances other than a disease or injury

ICD-9-CM provides codes to deal with encounters for circumstances other than a disease or injury. The Supplementary Classification of factors Influencing Health Status and Contact with Health Services (V01.0- V91.99) is provided to deal with occasions when circumstances other than a disease or injury are recorded as diagnosis or problems. *See Section I.C. 18 for information on V-codes.*

G. Level of Detail in Coding

1. ICD-9-CM codes with 3, 4, or 5 digits

ICD-9-CM is composed of codes with either 3, 4, or 5 digits. Codes with three digits are included in ICD-9-CM as the heading of a category of codes that may be further subdivided by the use of fourth and/or fifth digits, which provide greater specificity.

2. Use of full number of digits required for a code

A three-digit code is to be used only if it is not further subdivided. Where fourth-digit subcategories and/or fifth-digit subclassifications are provided, they must be assigned. A code is invalid if it has not been coded to the full number of digits required for that code.
See also discussion under Section I.b.3., General Coding Guidelines, Level of Detail in Coding.

H. ICD-9-CM code for the diagnosis, condition, problem, or other reason for encounter/visit

List first the ICD-9-CM code for the diagnosis, condition, problem, or other reason for encounter/visit shown in the medical record to be chiefly responsible for the services provided. List additional codes that describe any coexisting conditions. In some cases the first-listed diagnosis may be a symptom when a diagnosis has not been established (confirmed) by the physician.

I. Uncertain diagnosis

Do not code diagnoses documented as "probable", "suspected," "questionable," "rule out," or "working diagnosis" or other similar terms indicating uncertainty. Rather, code the condition(s) to the highest degree of certainty for that encounter/visit, such as symptoms, signs, abnormal test results, or other reason for the visit.

Please note: This differs from the coding practices used by short-term, acute care, long-term care and psychiatric hospitals.

J. Chronic diseases

Chronic diseases treated on an ongoing basis may be coded and reported as many times as the patient receives treatment and care for the condition(s)

K. Code all documented conditions that coexist

Code all documented conditions that coexist at the time of the encounter/visit, and require or affect patient care treatment or management. Do not code conditions that were previously treated and no longer exist. However, history codes (V10-V19) may be used as secondary codes if the historical condition or family history has an impact on current care or influences treatment.

L. Patients receiving diagnostic services only

For patients receiving diagnostic services only during an encounter/visit, sequence first the diagnosis, condition, problem, or other reason for encounter/visit shown in the medical record to be chiefly responsible for the outpatient services provided during the encounter/visit. Codes for other diagnoses (e.g., chronic conditions) may be sequenced as additional diagnoses.

For encounters for routine laboratory/radiology testing in the absence of any signs, symptoms, or associated diagnosis, assign V72.5 and/or a code from subcategory V72.6. If routine testing is performed during the same encounter as a test to evaluate a sign, symptom, or diagnosis, it is appropriate to assign both the V code and the code describing the reason for the non-routine test.

For outpatient encounters for diagnostic tests that have been interpreted by a physician, and the final report is available at the time of coding, code any confirmed or definitive diagnosis(es) documented in the interpretation. Do not code related signs and symptoms as additional diagnoses.

Please note: This differs from the coding practice in the hospital inpatient setting regarding abnormal findings on test results.

M. Patients receiving therapeutic services only

For patients receiving therapeutic services only during an encounter/visit, sequence first the diagnosis, condition, problem, or other reason for encounter/visit shown in the medical record to be chiefly responsible for the outpatient services provided during the encounter/visit. Codes for other diagnoses (e.g., chronic conditions) may be sequenced as additional diagnoses.

The only exception to this rule is that when the primary reason for the admission/encounter is chemotherapy, radiation therapy, or rehabilitation, the appropriate V code for the service is listed first, and the diagnosis or problem for which the service is being performed listed second.

N. Patients receiving preoperative evaluations only

For patients receiving preoperative evaluations only, sequence first a code from category V72.8, Other specified examinations, to describe the pre-op consultations. Assign a code for the condition to describe the reason for the surgery as an additional diagnosis. Code also any findings related to the pre-op evaluation.

O. Ambulatory surgery

For ambulatory surgery, code the diagnosis for which the surgery was performed. If the postoperative diagnosis is known to be different from the preoperative diagnosis at the time the diagnosis is confirmed, select the postoperative diagnosis for coding, since it is the most definitive.

P. Routine outpatient prenatal visits

For routine outpatient prenatal visits when no complications are present, codes V22.0, Supervision of normal first pregnancy, or V22.1, Supervision of other normal pregnancy, should be used as the principal diagnosis. These codes should not be used in conjunction with chapter 11 codes.

The Ten Commandments of ICD-9-CM Diagnosis Coding

An irreverent summary of rules with practical coding hints

I. The largest number of digits wins.

   Do not report 3 if there are 4, do not report 4 if there are 5.

II. Numeric codes win over alphanumeric.

   If the condition is listed twice, once beginning with a letter and once with all numbers, use the one with all numbers, if possible.

III. Watch out for punctuation.

   Do not even think it. Do not think "427 point 0" or "250 point 00." These codes are 4270 and 25000. Many claim form scanners and electronic claim programs cannot process the punctuation mark correctly.

IV. Use only the code(s) related to the services performed.

   A patient with acute bronchitis and heart disease is seen for the bronchitis. The chart indicates it is time for an ECG. If you code the ECG for bronchitis, it may not pay. With Medicare, it could result in a "not medically necessary" rejection.

V. Diagnosis coding does not raise the payment, only allows it.

   A "better" diagnosis will not raise the payment. The neck can be x-rayed for pain, arthritis, or cervical fracture: all will allow payment. The diagnosis of foot pain, even if treated at this office visit, does not justify a neck x-ray.

VI. Do not code in greater specificity than the information provided.

   Do not code "rule out" and "suspected" as if the condition existed. The patient is seen because she thinks she broke her hand. If related to an accident and when the x-ray does not confirm a fracture, code "pain" or "contusion" or "traumatic injury."

VII. Neoplasms are always benign, unless stated to be malignant. If malignant, they are always primary, unless stated to be secondary or in situ.

   Some lesion codes are general, others are found in the neoplasm table. When using the table, be certain to select the correct column and verify that code with the Tabular List. Do not give the patient something he does not have, and cannot be documented as treated.

VIII. Always verify codes selected from the Alphabetic Index with the Tabular List.

IX. Diagnosis codes in the Tabular List, in italics, cannot be used as the primary diagnosis.

   These codes are listed as "excludes" or appear in italics stating "code first the underlying disease." Be certain the correct code is selected and verified.

X. Sometimes the best diagnosis code is going to be the one that is least incorrect.

Moving from ICD-9-CM to ICD-10-CM

On October 1, 2013, health care providers using ICD-9-CM must begin reporting diagnoses from ICD-10-CM. CMS reports that there will be no delay in implementation since they first released information about this change in 2007. This change in the coding process will amount to an expensive transition for providers, estimated at $99 million, $293 million, and $1.2 billion for small, medium, and large practices, respectively. But they are not alone. In September 2010, America's Health Insurance Plans (AHIP) estimated that costs of transition could reach $2 to $3 billion for insurers.

ICD-10-CM has over 69,000 codes; ICD-9-CM has under 15,000. ICD-10-CM has 21 chapters; ICD-9-CM has 19. ICD-10-CM codes are all alphanumeric; ICD-9-CM has only numeric codes except for the E and V codes. ICD-10-CM codes are 3 to 7 characters in length; ICD-9-CM codes are 3 to 5 characters long. ICD-10-CM may require "building" the code from more than one table; ICD-9-CM uses single tables for building codes.

If you presently code from ICD-9-CM for diagnoses and CPT® for procedures, you will continue to use CPT with ICD-10-CM. If you currently code from ICD-9-CM Volume 3 (Procedures), you will use ICD-10-CM/PCS. Because ICD-10-CM has not yet been printed in its final form, which is expected to become available in 2012, the following information comes from the 2011 draft publication of ICD-10-CM.

CMS announced a partial freeze on code changes prior to the implementation of ICD-10-CM on October 1, 2013. Code changes will be made only to capture new technology and new diseases. The timetable is as follows:

Date	ICD-9-CM	ICD-10-CM
10/01/2011	Last regular annual update	Last regular annual update
10/01/2012	Limited updates	Limited updates
10/01/2013	Terminated	Becomes the coding standard
10/01/2014		Regular annual updates begin

ICD-10-CM has guidelines for reporting but the rules are more complex than the guidelines of ICD-9-CM. The coder will need a greater understanding of anatomy, physiology, and terminology to code correctly in ICD-10-CM. These guideline sections are as follows:

Section I: Conventions, general coding guidelines, and chapter-specific guidelines

Section II: Selection of principal diagnosis

Section III: Reporting additional diagnoses

Section IV: Diagnostic coding and reporting guidelines for outpatient services

Generally, Sections II and III are used for hospital reporting. Sections I and IV will be used most frequently by the physician's office coder.

Chapter-specific guidelines appear in Section I but have not yet been developed for the following:

D50-D89	Diseases of Blood and Blood-Organs and Certain Disorders Involving the Immune Mechanism
H00-H59	Diseases of the Eye and Adnexa
H60-H95	Diseases of the Ear and Mastoid Process
K00-K94	Diseases of the Digestive System

There are significant notes at the start of each chapter in ICD-10-CM specifying how those codes are to be used. These instructions clarify many scenarios that have caused problems for coders over the years. While ICD-10-CM requires more precise coding, we are given additional directions for selecting the correct code.

Each chapter begins with information on what is included; what codes are never reported together (Excludes1); and the conditions that are not included in the code but may be reported with that code if both conditions exist (Excludes2). There is also a breakdown of the code blocks in that chapter, such as:

D00-D09	In situ neoplasms	P10-P15	Birth trauma	V00-X58	Accidents
K40-K46	Hernias	S80-S89	Injuries to the knee and lower leg	X92-Y08	Assault

The following table compares ICD-9-CM chapters with the chapters in ICD-10-CM:

ICD-9-CM Chapter/Name	Code Range	ICD-10-CM Chapter/Name	Code Range
1. Infectious and Parasitic Diseases	001–139	1. Certain Infectious and Parasitic Diseases	A00–B99
2. Neoplasms	140–239	2. Neoplasms	C00-D49
3. Endocrine, Nutritional, and Metabolic Diseases, and Immunity Disorders	240–279	3. Diseases of the Blood and Blood-forming Organs and Certain Disorders Involving the Immune Mechanism	D50-D89
4. Disease of Blood and Blood Forming Organs	280–289	4. Endocrine, Nutritional, and Metabolic Diseases	E00–E89
5. Mental Disorders	290–319	5. Mental and Behavioral Disorders	F01–F99
6. Diseases of Nervous System and Sense Organs	320–389	6. Diseases of the Nervous System	G00–G99
7. Diseases of Circulatory System	390–459	7. Diseases of the Eye and Adnexa	H00–H59
8. Diseases of Respiratory System	460–519	8. Diseases of the Ear and Mastoid Process	H60–H95
9. Diseases of Digestive System	520–579	9. Diseases of the Circulatory System	I00–I99
10. Diseases of the Genitourinary System	580–629	10. Disease of the Respiratory System	J00–J99
11. Complications of Pregnancy, Childbirth, and Puerperium	630–679	11. Diseases of the Digestive System	K00–K94
12. Diseases of Skin and Subcutaneous Tissue	680–709	12. Diseases of the Skin and Subcutaneous Tissue	L00-L99
13. Diseases of Musculoskeletal and Connective Tissue	710–739	13. Diseases of the Musculoskeletal System and Connective Tissue	M00–M99
14. Congenital Anomalies	740–759	14. Diseases of the Genitourinary System	N00–N99
15. Certain Conditions Originating in the Perinatal Period	760–779	15. Pregnancy, Childbirth, and the Puerperium	O00-O9a
16. Signs, Symptoms, and Ill-Defined Conditions	780–799	16. Certain Conditions Originating in the Perinatal Period	P00–P96
17. Injury and Poisoning	800-999	17. Congenital Malformations, Deformations, and Chromosomal Abnormalities	Q00–Q99
18. Classification of Factors Influencing Health Status and Contact with Health Service	V01-V91	18. Symptoms, Signs, and Abnormal Clinical and Laboratory Findings, Not Elsewhere Classified	R00–R99
19. Supplemental Classification of External Causes of Injury and Poisoning	E000-E999	19. Injury, Poisoning, and Certain Other Consequences of External Causes	S00–T88
		20. External Causes of Morbidity	V00–Y99
		21. Factors Influencing Health Status and Contact with Health Services	Z00–Z99

65

All ICD-10-CM codes are alphanumeric; only the V and E codes of ICD-9-CM contain letters. There are 3 to 7 characters in the new coding system, where ICD-9-CM had 3 to 5.

ICD-10-CM uses all letters except "U" as the first character:

Character	2	Numeric
	3	Alpha or numeric (not case sensitive)
	4–7	Alpha or numeric (not case sensitive); (may have an "x" as a place holder in positions 4–6)

The code will be invalid if the x's are omitted. All codes requiring a seventh character must include an x or xx unless the code is already 6 characters in length. The seventh character of the code gives specific information about the encounter or the medical condition. It must appear in the seventh position. The x is a placeholder, to allow for the proper number of characters.

The seventh character may indicate that this is an initial encounter for this condition (A); that this is a subsequent encounter for fracture with delayed healing (G); or that this encounter is for the sequela of a condition (S). If this key information appears in any other position but the seventh, important data will be missing and therefore the code will be invalid. Code S82 ("Fracture of the lower leg, including ankle") has 16 different letters for the seventh position. There are also notes stating that some of the 16 characters do not apply to certain subcategories of S82 (see "Fracture of the patella," S82.0).

Since the place holder is not case sensitive, you may wish to use lower case for readability, as these are complex code configurations:

S61.022A	Initial encounter for a laceration with foreign body of left thumb without damage to nail
S77.02xA	Initial encounter for a crushing injury to the left hip
Y36.6x0S	Sequelae of war operations involving biological weapons encountered as a military personnel

Computer systems convert lower case letters to upper case for health care claims. If you haven't stopped using the lower case L for 1 (one) or continue to use the capital O for the number 0 (zero), get out of that habit now as this will create invalid codes when reporting in ICD-10-CM.

Organizations are introducing special references and online courses to provide a greater understanding of anatomy, physiology, and terminology described and used in ICD-10-CM. These may be especially helpful if you code from operative reports where the physician's terminology may not match the terms used in the coding system.

This material was prepared with the 2011 Draft of ICD-10-CM. The 2012 Draft will be available in February 2012. There may be another Draft in October 2012, and the final ICD-10-CM should be released in time for the 10-1-2013 implementation date. Since codes are frozen in 2012, the release of updates in October 2012 may not be a full printing of ICD-10-CM but an addendum to the 2012 Draft.

Coding Conflicts

It is not clear (yet) whether a claim will be rejected when a procedure code and modifiers do not match the new diagnosis coding structure. It is easy to see how this could occur.

Example 1:

Procedure:	Hallux valgus, right, Silver: 28290-T5
ICD-10-CM:	Hallux valgus (acquired), unspecified foot
	M20.11: Hallux valgus (acquired), right foot
	M20.12: Hallux valgus (acquired), left foot

Selecting a diagnosis code other than M20.11 will be incorrect. Will the claim be rejected? We don't know.

Example 2:

Procedure:	Excise chalazion, right lower lid: 67800-RT or 67800-E4
ICD-10-CM:	H00.11: Chalazion, right upper eyelid
	H00.12: Chalazion, right lower eyelid
	H00.13: Chalazion, right eye, unspecified eyelid
	H00.14: Chalazion, left upper eyelid
	H00.15: Chalazion, left lower eyelid
	H00.16: Chalazion, left eye, unspecified eyelid
	H00.19: Chalazion, unspecified eye, unspecified eyelid

All these are incorrect diagnoses except H00.12. Let's hope our medical record documentation never results in having to select H00.19.

Will claims be rejected when we report a second initial encounter for the same condition reported last week? Will there be problems from reporting too many "unspecified" diagnoses? At present, we do not know the answers to these questions. If we learn to code accurately in ICD-10-CM, we will never need to consider these possible problems.

Diagnosis Coding Worksheet Instructions

This workbook divides diagnosis codes by chapters, each with two worksheets. Exercise I requires the use of the Tabular List. Study the code section of the Tabular List and record the appropriate THREE-DIGIT category indicator for where you would find that condition listed. Your search may be easier if you look in the ICD-9-CM Appendix E for the three-digit categories. Then go to the Tabular section for verification of your choice. Always read the introductory notes at the beginning of each section to find the basic rules for the codes in that category.

The second exercise requires a search of the Alphabetic Index and verification of the code in the Tabular volume. Some diagnosis codes require a fifth digit that may not be easy to find in the Alphabetic Index.

Take the time to look around the reference volumes as you use them. Some of the worksheet codes have very unusual codes listed near them. Would you believe there is a diagnosis called "no room at the inn"? Can you guess what it means? Look it up and see if you were right.

The workbook now includes a column for the ICD-9-CM and ICD-10-CM codes. Perhaps you have one of the ICD-9-CM references for 2011 that contains pointers to the corresponding code section in ICD-10-CM. You will need access to the ICD-10-CM draft codebook to find these codes. Because ICD-10-CM has 21 chapters while ICD-9-CM has 19, some of the worksheet items may be found in other sections of ICD-10-CM. Also, some conditions in sections of ICD-9-CM appear in other chapters in ICD-10-CM. The ICD-10-CM "Draft Official Guidelines for Coding and Reporting" are included in the draft coding reference. Instructions and conventions in the code classification sections take precedence over these general guidelines.

Because these codes come from the draft codebook, they may change when the final coding reference is released. The final ICD-10-CM will likely maintain the general structure of the chapters, sections, and diagnosis codes in the draft. Always read the instructions found at the start of each ICD-10-CM chapter for the Includes, Excludes1, and Excludes2 notes as well as the identifying blocks, where certain conditions can be found.

ICD-10-CM codes have up to 7 characters, 2 more than the maximum number in ICD-9-CM. The listed code may have only 4 or 5 characters and include a table for the 7th character. In those instances, you must insert the correct number of x's (placeholders) to be certain the 7th character appears in the 7th position. An initial encounter for code T28.1 would be reported as T28.1xxA. The x does not need to be entered in lower case but is used to make the code easier to read: T28.1xxA, rather than T28.1XXA. Also note that some codes appearing close in ICD-9-CM, such as 625.4 and 625.5, become in ICD-10-CM codes N94.3 and N94.89.

Assume all worksheet items are the "initial encounter" unless stated otherwise, such as "follow up" or "sequelae."

Answers to the Reasonableness Test:

1. Diagnosis: 5, 6, 7, 8, 13, 16
   Procedure: 1, 4, 11, 12, 13, 15, 17

2. Diagnosis: 8, 16, 17
   Procedure: 1, 5, 15, 16, 17

3. Gotcha! There isn't enough information here to code this one correctly. Is it a skin ulcer, mouth ulcer, or abdominal ulcer? Identify all the ulcer types you can think of, and code them all for diagnoses and procedures.

Name _____

Infectious/Parasitic Diseases – I (001–139)

2012 ICD-9-CM and ICD-10-CM

These diseases are generally considered communicable or transmissible. Also included are a few diseases of unknown or possibly infectious origin. You must use caution with these codes, as they can affect employment possibilities, such as identifying a communicable disease for a food handler, a cook, or a waiter. A person's ability to obtain life or health insurance can be affected by a report of one of these diseases, and there could be other significant consequences. This section contains the codes for AIDS, ARC, and HIV used to register patients with the Centers for Disease Control and Prevention (CDC).

Additionally, an incorrectly reported diagnosis can indicate that a condition was diagnosed but never treated. There would be no documentation supporting referral or therapy for the misdiagnosis. This could also raise malpractice issues of failure to treat or abandonment.

ICD-10-CM: Certain Infectious and Parasitic Diseases - A00–B99

Refer to Chapter 1 for extensive general coding guidelines for HIV and sepsis. The diseases discussed in this chapter are generally recognized as communicable or transmissible.

Using the Tabular List only, identify the three-digit category for the following:

		ICD-9-CM	ICD-10-CM
1.	Salmonella infection	_____	_____
2.	Acute viral hepatitis	_____	_____
3.	Sequelae of polio	_____	_____
4.	TB of central nervous system	_____	_____
5.	Herpes simplex	_____	_____
6.	Mumps	_____	_____
7.	Trench mouth	_____	_____
8.	HIV	_____	_____
9.	Chlamydial vaginitis	_____	_____
10.	Warts	_____	_____

Name _____

Infectious/Parasitic Diseases – II (001–139)

Using the alphabetic and/or tabular references, locate the following conditions and code to acceptable specificity, 3 to 7 characters.

		ICD-9-CM	ICD-10-CM
1.	Acute viral conjunctivitis from swimming pool	_____	_____
2.	Coma from bite of rabid dog	_____	_____
3.	Seven-day Queensland fever	_____	_____
4.	Lyme disease	_____	_____
5.	Ringworm	_____	_____
6.	Trichomonal fluor	_____	_____
7.	Congenital syphilitic saddle nose	_____	_____
8.	Echovirus intestinal infection	_____	_____
9.	Dandy fever	_____	_____
10.	Ground itch	_____	_____
11.	Group A shigellosis	_____	_____
12.	Haverhill streptobacillus	_____	_____
13.	Pseudocowpox	_____	_____
14.	Subacute spongiform encephalopathy	_____	_____
15.	Paratyphoid fever	_____	_____
16.	Rubella encephalitis	_____	_____
17.	Australian X disease	_____	_____
18.	Pulmonary paracoccidioidomycosis	_____	_____
19.	Anaerobic sepsis	_____	_____
20.	Schaumann's lymphogranulomatosis	_____	_____
21.	Early macular leprosy, Group 1	_____	_____
22.	Lupus tuberculosis	_____	_____
23.	Ebola viral fever	_____	_____
24.	African eyeworm infection	_____	_____
25.	Monkey malaria	_____	_____

Name _____

Neoplasms - I (140–239)

2012 ICD-9-CM and ICD-10-CM

Coders frequently have trouble with neoplasms. Accuracy is critical if the doctor plans to enroll the patient in one of the cancer registry services. A Johns-Hopkins representative told of finding that over 50% of the patients in their tumor registry did not have the cancer specified in their enrollment records. Referring physician errors on the registration documents caused Johns-Hopkins to send the doctor's information on treating the wrong kind of tumor.

Read the instructions for this section very carefully. The Alphabetic Index contains a neoplasm table. This is the starting place when you look for a neoplasm code. The table has separate codes for primary, secondary, and CA in situ. The Tabular List arranges the codes by body site, in a similar sequence as the neoplasm table. As a general practice, avoid coding "uncertain behavior" and "unspecified" unless you have a pathology report that uses those terms. Hold the claim until you know the type of neoplasm. If you code malignant, and it is benign, it may be very difficult to get the records changed. If you code benign and it is malignant, you may not receive the correct payment.

Caution: There is a "trick" question on the worksheet. Read the instructions carefully!

ICD-10-CM: Neoplasms - C00–D49

In Chapter 2, there are many general coding guidelines for reporting malignancies and a note to query the provider to determine if the leukemia patient is in remission or has a personal history of leukemia. Use the neoplasm table first to find the code. However, if the documentation includes the histologic term, search on that term. All codes must be verified in the tabular. Note that C00–C75 codes are for malignant neoplasms and D00–D09 for in situ neoplasms; benign neoplasms start at D10. Many codes state use of additional code to identify a contributing cause. Use the additional codes only if documented in the medical record.

Using the Tabular List only, identify the three-digit category for the following:

		ICD-9-CM	ICD-10-CM
1.	Malignant neoplasm of tongue	_____	_____
2.	Benign neoplasm of tongue	_____	_____
3.	Skin carcinoma in situ	_____	_____
4.	Myeloid leukemia	_____	_____
5.	Malignant neoplasm of pancreas	_____	_____
6.	Kaposi's Sarcoma	_____	_____
7.	Breast carcinoma in situ	_____	_____
8.	Benign brain tumor	_____	_____
9.	Lung malignancy	_____	_____
10.	Bladder cancer	_____	_____

Neoplasms - II (140–239)

Using the alphabetic and/or tabular references, locate the following conditions and code to acceptable specificity, 3 to 7 characters.

		ICD-9-CM	ICD-10-CM
1.	Cardia carcinoma	_____	_____
2.	Primary cancer of the cauda equina	_____	_____
3.	Cancer of the lip border	_____	_____
4.	Carcinoma in situ, thalamus	_____	_____
5.	Tumor of coccyx, secondary to brain cancer	_____	_____
6.	Dermatofibroma, skin of the abdominal wall	_____	_____
7.	Cancer of the brain	_____	_____
8.	Metastasis to Zuckerkandl's organ	_____	_____
9.	Unspecified tumor of Cowper's gland	_____	_____
10.	Benign tumor of the left eyebrow	_____	_____
11.	Metastatic carcinoma of the omentum	_____	_____
12.	Uterine malignancy	_____	_____
13.	Benign neoplasm right renal pelvis	_____	_____
14.	Polycythemia vera	_____	_____
15.	Mesocolonic malignancy	_____	_____
16.	Pancreatic duct cancer	_____	_____
17.	Lymphangioendothelioma, benign	_____	_____
18.	Malignant neoplasm of submaxillary gland	_____	_____
19.	Tracheal carcinoma in situ	_____	_____
20.	Benign tumor of thymus	_____	_____
21.	Non-Hodgkin's lymphoma, left axillary nodes	_____	_____
22.	Benign tumor of breast, male	_____	_____
23.	Cancer of the lower respiratory system	_____	_____
24.	Retrobulbar malignancy, left eye	_____	_____
25.	Glossopalatine fold carcinoma	_____	_____

Name _____

Endocrine, Nutritional, Metabolic, Immunity Disorders - I (240–279)

2012 ICD-9-CM and ICD-10-CM

This section deals with diseases NOT caused by tumor. These are some of the most common reasons for a visit to the doctor's office. Many of these conditions are hereditary, many last a lifetime. Many contribute to health complications as we age. As a wise man once said, "Most people die of the cumulative effects of heredity, lifestyle, and environment."

ICD-10-CM: Endocrine, Nutritional, and Metabolic Diseases - E00–E89

Chapter 4 coding guidelines provide information on identifying diabetes as Type 1 or Type 2. Review the "Includes" and "Excludes" for this chapter. Also, a very common disease in this ICD-9-CM chapter has been reclassified to another section of ICD-10-CM.

Using the Tabular List only, identify the three-digit category for the following:

		ICD-9-CM	ICD-10-CM
1.	Hyperlipidemia	_____	_____
2.	Diabetes, Type 2	_____	_____
3.	Thyrotoxicosis	_____	_____
4.	Vitamin D deficiency	_____	_____
5.	Dwarfism	_____	_____
6.	Obesity	_____	_____
7.	Beriberi	_____	_____
8.	Testicular dysfunction	_____	_____
9.	Acute thyroid disease	_____	_____
10.	Gout	_____	_____

Endocrine, Nutritional, Metabolic, Immunity Disorders - II (240–279)

Using the alphabetic and/or tabular references, locate the following conditions and code to acceptable specificity, 3 to 7 characters.

		ICD-9-CM	ICD-10-CM
1.	Proliferative Type 2 diabetic retinopathy		
2.	Addison's disease		
3.	Nutritional marasmus		
4.	Pickwickian syndrome		
5.	Glucoglycinuria		
6.	Hashimoto's disease		
7.	Ketoacidosis with coma, Type 1 diabetes		
8.	Lymphatism		
9.	Graves' disease with storm		
10.	Pendred's syndrome		
11.	Severe malnutrition from dieting		
12.	Scurvy		
13.	Pseudopseudohypoparathyroidism		
14.	Iatrogenic hyperinsulinism		
15.	Nezelof's syndrome		
16.	Delayed puberty		
17.	Lactose intolerance		
18.	Acute gout attack		
19.	Cushing's syndrome		
20.	Cystic fibrosis		
21.	Respiratory alkalosis		
22.	Alcoholic pellagra		
23.	Struma nodosa		
24.	Night blindness due to vitamin A deficiency		
25.	Acute rickets		

Name _____

Blood and Blood-Forming Organs - I (280–289)

2012 ICD-9-CM and ICD-10-CM

This section covers diseases of the blood and blood-forming organs. Anemia and clotting disorders are the most common.

ICD-10-CM: Diseases of the Blood and Blood-Forming Organs and Certain Disorders Involving the Immune Mechanism - D50–D89

No general guidelines have been developed for Chapter 3. Some immune system conditions previously listed in other chapters of ICD-9-CM are now in this chapter.

Note: One item has a code from another chapter.

Using the Tabular List only, identify the three-digit category for the following:

		ICD-9-CM	ICD-10-CM
1.	Christmas disease	_____	_____
2.	Cooley's anemia	_____	_____
3.	Infantile pseudoleukemia	_____	_____
4.	Marchiafava-Micheli syndrome	_____	_____
5.	Imerslund's syndrome	_____	_____
6.	Aplastic anemia NOS	_____	_____
7.	Hereditary hyposegmentation	_____	_____
8.	Sideropenic dysphagia	_____	_____
9.	Emotional polycythemia	_____	_____
10.	Megakaryocytic hypoplasia	_____	_____

Name _____

Blood and Blood-Forming Organs - II (280–289)

Using the alphabetic and/or tabular references, locate the following conditions and code to acceptable specificity, 3 to 7 characters.

		ICD-9-CM	ICD-10-CM
1.	Antithromboplastinemia	_____	_____
2.	Paroxysmal cold disease	_____	_____
3.	Massive blood transfusion thrombocytopenia	_____	_____
4.	Hypergammaglobulinemia	_____	_____
5.	Normocytic anemia	_____	_____
6.	Siderotic splenomegaly	_____	_____
7.	Chronic hemoglobin SS disease	_____	_____
8.	Plummer-Vinson disease	_____	_____
9.	Autoimmune cold anemia	_____	_____
10.	Iron deficiency anemia	_____	_____
11.	Blood dyscrasia	_____	_____
12.	Mechanical hemolytic anemia	_____	_____
13.	Vitamin K deficiency	_____	_____
14.	Lazy leukocyte syndrome	_____	_____
15.	Classical hemophilia	_____	_____
16.	Hemoglobinopathy	_____	_____
17.	Splenitis	_____	_____
18.	Sclerothymic hyperviscosity syndrome	_____	_____
19.	Idiopathic allergic eosinophilia	_____	_____
20.	Thrombocytopathy	_____	_____
21.	Thalassemic variants	_____	_____
22.	Blackfan-Diamond syndrome	_____	_____
23.	Lymphocytopenia	_____	_____
24.	Consumption coagulopathy	_____	_____
25.	Goat's milk anemia	_____	_____

Name _____

Mental Disorders - I (290–319)

2012 ICD-9-CM and ICD-10-CM

Read the introduction carefully. Notice the exclusion of diseases with an organic origin. This section includes psychoses, neuroses, conduct disorders, and retardation.

Caution: Worksheet item 20 on the next page.

ICD-10-CM: Mental and Behavioral Disorders - F01–F99

The 2011 draft contains only general guidelines for Chapter 5: Pain disorders and disorders due to psychoactive substance use.

Using the Tabular List only, identify the three-digit category for the following:

		ICD-9-CM	ICD-10-CM
1.	Neurasthenia	_____	_____
2.	Asperger's syndrome	_____	_____
3.	Paranoia	_____	_____
4.	Voyeurism	_____	_____
5.	Anorexia nervosa	_____	_____
6.	Schizophrenia	_____	_____
7.	Pyromania	_____	_____
8.	Dipsomania	_____	_____
9.	Korsakoff's non-alcoholic syndrome	_____	_____
10.	Bipolar disorder	_____	_____

Mental Disorders - II (290–319)

Name _____

Using the alphabetic and/or tabular references, locate the following conditions and code to acceptable specificity, 3 to 7 characters.

		ICD-9-CM	ICD-10-CM
1.	Hypochondriac		
2.	Organic brain syndrome		
3.	Panic agoraphobia		
4.	Insomnia from alcohol abuse		
5.	Munchausen's syndrome		
6.	Catatonic schizophrenia in remission		
7.	Pseudocyesis		
8.	IQ 27		
9.	Psychogenic polyarthralgia		
10.	Simple senile dementia		
11.	Hyperactive attention deficit disorder		
12.	Inherited profound idiocy		
13.	Moderate monopolar mania		
14.	Manic depressive bipolar disorder		
15.	Severe marijuana dependence anxiety		
16.	Occasional adjustment insomnia		
17.	Asexual transsexualism by history		
18.	Occasional cocaine abuse		
19.	Acute chronic paranoid schizophrenia		
20.	Frequent leader of 4th grade truancy group		
21.	Shoe fetish		
22.	Dyspraxic syndrome		
23.	Psychogenic dyspareunia		
24.	Subacute infective psychosis		
25.	Active Heller's syndrome		

Name _____

Nervous System and Sense Organs - I (320–389)

2012 ICD-9-CM and ICD-10-CM

Inflammatory, hereditary, and degenerative diseases of the central nervous system, as well as disorders of the peripheral nervous system, eyes, and ears are included in this section. Review the table describing the levels of visual impairment and note the difference in the U.S. and WHO definitions of blindness.

Caution: two-word description may give you different codes depending on which word you look up in the alphabetic index. Either could be correct. Isn't that interesting?

ICD-10-CM: Diseases of the Nervous System and Sense Organs - G00–G99

      Diseases of the Eye and Adnexa - H00–H59

      Diseases of the Ear and Mastoid Process - H60–H95

Chapter 6 provides guidelines for coding the G codes but there are no general guidelines for the eye (Chapter 7) and ear (Chapter 8). Conditions specified as "right" or "left" will have different diagnosis codes, as will "dominant" and "non-dominant." Usually the right is listed before the left but "unspecified" may be listed before the "right" code or after the code listed as "left." There are also separate codes for bilateral, as well as codes to indicate the upper or lower eyelid.

The code for the external cause, if documented in the medical record, is listed after the code for the eye or ear condition.

Note the important Excludes2 for each of these sections.

Using the Tabular List only, identify the three-digit category for the following:

		ICD-9-CM	ICD-10-CM
1.	Hemophilus meningitis	_____	_____
2.	Pick's disease	_____	_____
3.	Senile cataract	_____	_____
4.	Pseudocyst of the retina	_____	_____
5.	Double vision	_____	_____
6.	Otitis media	_____	_____
7.	Restless legs	_____	_____
8.	Meniere's disease	_____	_____
9.	Keratoconus	_____	_____
10.	Tic douloureux	_____	_____

Nervous System and Sense Organs - II (320–389)

Name _____

Using the alphabetic and/or tabular reference, locate the following conditions and code to acceptable specificity, 3 to 7 characters.

		ICD-9-CM	ICD-10-CM
1.	Retrolental fibroplasia, bilateral	_____	_____
2.	Friedlander bacterial meningitis	_____	_____
3.	Friedreich's ataxia	_____	_____
4.	Postimmunization encephalitis	_____	_____
5.	Primary central sleep apnea	_____	_____
6.	Hereditary macular corneal dystrophy	_____	_____
7.	Mastoid cholesteatoma, left	_____	_____
8.	Familial tremor	_____	_____
9.	Arcus senilis, right	_____	_____
10.	Multiple sclerosis	_____	_____
11.	Guillain-Barre syndrome	_____	_____
12.	Bilateral vitreous floaters	_____	_____
13.	Jamaican neuropathy	_____	_____
14.	Amaurosis, both eyes	_____	_____
15.	Morton's neuroma, left	_____	_____
16.	Decreased ocular pressure with papilledema	_____	_____
17.	Reye's syndrome	_____	_____
18.	Romberg's syndrome	_____	_____
19.	Obstructive hydrocephalus	_____	_____
20.	Bell's palsy	_____	_____
21.	Pseudohole of the macula, left	_____	_____
22.	Tympanosclerosis	_____	_____
23.	Pars planitis	_____	_____
24.	Crossed eyes, alternating A pattern	_____	_____
25.	Soemmering's ring, left eye	_____	_____

Name _____

Circulatory System - I (390–459)

2012 ICD-9-CM and ICD-10-CM

This system includes rheumatic fever and resulting heart disease, hypertensive and ischemic heart disease, diseases of the pulmonary circulation, and other heart diseases. It also includes cerebrovascular disease and diseases of the blood vessels and lymphatics.

ICD-10-CM: Diseases of the Circulatory System - I00–I99

Chapter 9 general guidelines explain selection of codes for hypertension, acute myocardial infarction, atherosclerosis, angina, and cerebrovascular disease.

Five worksheet items come from other sections of ICD-10-CM. Do you see the pattern to these changes?

Using the Tabular List only, identify the three-digit category for the following:

		ICD-9-CM	ICD-10-CM
1.	Septic pulmonary embolus	_____	_____
2.	Ruptured abdominal aortic aneurysm	_____	_____
3.	Myocardiopathy	_____	_____
4.	Mobitz II block	_____	_____
5.	Elephantiasis	_____	_____
6.	Postphlebitic syndrome	_____	_____
7.	Rendu-Osler-Weber disease	_____	_____
8.	Buerger's disease	_____	_____
9.	Arteriosclerosis	_____	_____
10.	Thrombosed hemorrhoids	_____	_____

Circulatory System - II (390-459)

Using the alphabetic and/or tabular references, locate the following conditions and code to acceptable specificity, 3 to 7 characters.

		ICD-9-CM	ICD-10-CM
1.	Sick sinus syndrome		
2.	Acute anterolateral myocardial infarct		
3.	Kawasaki disease		
4.	Subacute bacterial endocarditis		
5.	Heart failure with hypertension		
6.	Ruptured berry aneurysm		
7.	Bifascicular block		
8.	Temporal arteritis		
9.	Acute rheumatic endocarditis		
10.	Bilateral stenosis of carotid artery		
11.	Superior vena cava syndrome		
12.	Iliac vein phlebitis, left		
13.	Rare African cardiomyopathy		
14.	Benign secondary renovascular hypertension		
15.	Atrial flutter		
16.	Rheumatic aortic incompetence		
17.	Subclavian steal syndrome		
18.	Transient ischemic attacks		
19.	Stasis dermatitis		
20.	Transient global amnesia		
21.	Non-filarial chylocele		
22.	Intermittent claudication		
23.	Wolff-Parkinson-White disorder		
24.	Atherosclerosis of coronary artery bypass graft		
25.	Prinzmetal angina		

Respiratory System - I (460–519)

2012 ICD-9-CM and ICD-10-CM

This system includes acute infections and other respiratory diseases such as pneumonia and influenza, obstructive pulmonary disease, and external causes of lung disease, as well as other forms of lung disorders.

ICD-10-CM: Diseases of the Respiratory System - J00–J99

General guidelines for Chapter 10 provide information on coding asthma, COPD, and influenza. ICD-10-CM has eliminated many of the ICD-9-CM instructions on coding COPD.

One worksheet item code comes from a different chapter.

Using the Tabular List only, identify the three-digit category for the following:

		ICD-9-CM	ICD-10-CM
1.	Hay fever		
2.	Hemothorax		
3.	Aspiration pneumonia		
4.	Mucopurulent chronic bronchitis		
5.	Acute laryngitis		
6.	Bronchopneumonia		
7.	Mediastinitis		
8.	Pigeon fanciers' disease		
9.	Sinus polyp		
10.	Hemophilus pneumonia		

Name _____

Respiratory System - II (460–519)

Using the alphabetic and/or tabular references, locate the following conditions and code to acceptable specificity, 3 to 7 characters.

		ICD-9-CM	ICD-10-CM
1.	H1N1 influenza with pneumonia	_____	_____
2.	Traumatic nasal septal deflection	_____	_____
3.	Idiopathic diffuse interstitial fibrosis	_____	_____
4.	Retropharyngeal abscess	_____	_____
5.	Broncholithiasis	_____	_____
6.	Acute sinus infection	_____	_____
7.	Cork handlers' disease	_____	_____
8.	Tracheostenosis	_____	_____
9.	Postoperative pneumothorax	_____	_____
10.	Croup	_____	_____
11.	Allergic rhinitis	_____	_____
12.	Radiation fibrosis of the lung	_____	_____
13.	E. colipneumonia	_____	_____
14.	Laryngeal muscle spasm	_____	_____
15.	Black lung disease	_____	_____
16.	Eosinophilic asthma	_____	_____
17.	Acute gangrenous pharyngitis	_____	_____
18.	Chronic obstructive pulmonary disease	_____	_____
19.	Acute follicular tonsillitis	_____	_____
20.	Acute fistular empyema	_____	_____
21.	Legionnaire's disease	_____	_____
22.	Bullous emphysema	_____	_____
23.	Coryza, acute	_____	_____
24.	Chlamydial pneumonia	_____	_____
25.	Asthmatic bronchitis	_____	_____

Name _____

Digestive System - I (520–579)

2012 ICD-9-CM and ICD-10-CM

This unit covers diseases of the oral cavity, salivary glands and jaws, esophagus, stomach and duodenum; appendicitis; abdominal hernias; non-infectious enteritis and colitis; and other diseases of the intestines, peritoneum, and digestive system.

ICD-10-CM: Diseases of the Digestive System - K00–K94

The general guidelines for Chapter 11 coding will be developed at a later date. Medical record documentation should be reviewed for information on complications, acute/chronic conditions, and the specific site of abscesses.

One worksheet item code comes from a different chapter.

Using the Tabular List only, identify the three-digit category for the following:

		ICD-9-CM	ICD-10-CM
1.	Alcoholic cirrhosis	_____	_____
2.	Microdontia	_____	_____
3.	Cholecystitis	_____	_____
4.	Duodenal ulcer	_____	_____
5.	Sprue	_____	_____
6.	Pyloric stenosis	_____	_____
7.	Sialolithiasis	_____	_____
8.	Crohn's disease	_____	_____
9.	Pancreatitis	_____	_____
10.	Peritonitis, acute	_____	_____

Name _____

Digestive System - II (520–579)

Using the alphabetic and/or tabular reference, locate the following conditions and code to acceptable specificity, 3 to 7 characters.

		ICD-9-CM	ICD-10-CM
1.	Hematemesis	_____	_____
2.	Choledochoduodenal fistula	_____	_____
3.	Portal thrombophlebitis	_____	_____
4.	Pain in right TMJ	_____	_____
5.	Lingua villosa nigra	_____	_____
6.	Appendicitis with abscess	_____	_____
7.	Postgastrectomy diarrhea	_____	_____
8.	Teething syndrome	_____	_____
9.	Acute pyloric ulcer with hemorrhage	_____	_____
10.	Melena	_____	_____
11.	Recurrent gangrenous inguinal hernia	_____	_____
12.	Tooth discoloration from silver fillings	_____	_____
13.	Parotitis	_____	_____
14.	Glossodynia	_____	_____
15.	Sialodocholithiasis	_____	_____
16.	Diverticulosis of duodenum	_____	_____
17.	Nasolabial cyst	_____	_____
18.	Strangulated bowel	_____	_____
19.	Strawberry disease of the gallbladder	_____	_____
20.	Habitual tooth abrasion	_____	_____
21.	Retrocecal abscess	_____	_____
22.	Right femoral hernia	_____	_____
23.	Gastritis due to alcoholism	_____	_____
24.	Intussusception of appendix	_____	_____
25.	Chronic appendicitis	_____	_____

Name _____

Genitourinary System - I (580–629)

2012 ICD-9-CM and ICD-10-CM

This system includes diseases of the kidneys, bladder, ureters, urethra, and male genital organs. Also covered are the diseases of the breast, inflammatory conditions of the female pelvic organs, and female infertility.

Caution: Item 15 on the next page may be a challenge.

ICD-10-CM: Diseases of the Genitourinary System - N00–N99

Chapter 14 general guidelines provide information on coding chronic kidney disease. Some symptoms listed in ICD-9-CM "Symptoms/Signs" chapter, such as incontinence, have been moved to this chapter in ICD-10-CM. There is a note to "code also any associated kidney failure" and refers to codes N17-N19. The guidelines (Section 1, 17) state that "this note does not provide sequencing direction." However, N18 does state, "Code first any associated. . ." The Excludes2 should be familiar by now. You will find similar notes on code sequencing throughout the reference. Read them carefully.

Using the Tabular List only, identify the three-digit category for the following:

		ICD-9-CM	ICD-10-CM
1.	Moderate chronic kidney disease	_____	_____
2.	Paravaginal cystocele	_____	_____
3.	Acute prostatitis	_____	_____
4.	Fibrocystic breast	_____	_____
5.	Polymenorrhea	_____	_____
6.	Benign prostatic hypertrophy	_____	_____
7.	Uterine endometriosis	_____	_____
8.	Female infertility	_____	_____
9.	Male infertility	_____	_____
10.	Phimosis (congenital)	_____	_____

Name _____

Genitourinary System - II (580–629)

Using the alphabetic and/or tabular references, locate the following conditions and code to acceptable specificity, 3 to 7 characters.

		ICD-9-CM	ICD-10-CM
1.	Urinary tract infection (UTI)	_____	_____
2.	Posthysterectomy vaginal prolapse	_____	_____
3.	Gynecomastia	_____	_____
4.	Penile kraurosis	_____	_____
5.	Male infertility from radiation	_____	_____
6.	Salpingo-oophoritis	_____	_____
7.	Acute pelvic inflammatory disease	_____	_____
8.	Boil of the scrotum	_____	_____
9.	Rectovaginal endometriosis	_____	_____
10.	Breast lump	_____	_____
11.	Bartholin's gland cyst	_____	_____
12.	Chronic renal failure	_____	_____
13.	Cervical erosion	_____	_____
14.	Nephropathy NOS	_____	_____
15.	Overactive bladder	_____	_____
16.	Necrotizing glomerulonephritis	_____	_____
17.	Floating kidney	_____	_____
18.	Premenstrual syndrome	_____	_____
19.	Chocolate cyst of the ovary	_____	_____
20.	Chronic interstitial cystitis	_____	_____
21.	Balanitis	_____	_____
22.	Senile atrophic vaginitis	_____	_____
23.	Anovulatory infertility	_____	_____
24.	Urinary bladder stone	_____	_____
25.	Rupture of corpus luteum cyst	_____	_____

Name _____

Pregnancy, Childbirth, Puerperium - I (630–679)

2012 ICD-9-CM and ICD-10-CM

This unit includes conditions related to ectopic and molar pregnancy, abortive pregnancies, other pregnancy complications; normal delivery, other indications for pregnancy care, and labor and delivery; as well as complications of labor and delivery.

Caution: This is a complicated section. All Worksheet II terms must be checked with the Tabular List. Many codes have a required fifth digit. Note the limited options for the fifth digit.

ICD-10-CM: Pregnancy, Childbirth, and Puerperium - O00–O9a

The general guidelines for Chapter 15 provide information on reporting obstetric care, pre-existing conditions, and conditions of the fetus that affect the mother's care. These codes relate only to maternal records, and are never used on newborn records.

There is only one P (newborn) code on these worksheets; the rest relate to maternal conditions.

Using the Tabular List only, identify the three-digit category for the following:

		ICD-9-CM	ICD-10-CM
1.	Hemorrhoids from pregnancy	_____	_____
2.	ABO isoimmunization of newborn	_____	_____
3.	Ovarian pregnancy	_____	_____
4.	Hyperemesis gravidarum	_____	_____
5.	Fetopelvic disproportion	_____	_____
6.	Cord prolapse	_____	_____
7.	Transient hypertension of pregnancy	_____	_____
8.	Uterine rupture during labor	_____	_____
9.	Twin pregnancy	_____	_____
10.	Obesity complicating pregnancy	_____	_____

Name _____

Pregnancy, Childbirth, Puerperium - II (630–679)

Using the alphabetic and/or tabular references, locate the following conditions and code to acceptable specificity, 3 to 7 characters.

		ICD-9-CM	ICD-10-CM
1.	Severe antepartum thrombophlebitis	_____	O22.30
2.	Early separation of the placenta	_____	O45.001
3.	Incomplete spontaneous abortion with shock	_____	O03.31
4.	Eclampsia with convulsions	_____	O15.00
5.	Delivery of sextuplets	_____	O30.8??
6.	Suppressed lactation	_____	_____
7.	Reopening of recent C-section wound	_____	_____
8.	Obstetric shock during delivery	_____	_____
9.	Cardiac arrest from anesthesia for delivery	_____	_____
10.	Failed attempted abortion with hemorrhage	_____	_____
11.	Postpartum hemorrhage from retained placenta	_____	_____
12.	Ruptured fallopian tubal pregnancy	_____	_____
13.	Prenatal gestational edema	_____	_____
14.	Gonorrhea, seventh month of pregnancy	_____	_____
15.	Vaginal hematoma from delivery	_____	_____
16.	Preexisting benign essential hypertension with pregnancy	_____	_____
17.	Antepartum renal disease	_____	_____
18.	Fetopelvic disproportion obstructing labor	_____	_____
19.	Threatened abortion	_____	_____
20.	Maternal care and delivery for fetal death in utero	_____	_____
21.	Labor complicated by septicemia	_____	_____
22.	Missed abortion	_____	_____
23.	Spontaneous breech delivery	_____	_____
24.	Nursing mother mastitis	_____	_____
25.	Kidney shutdown following elective pregnancy termination	_____	_____

Name _____

Skin and Subcutaneous Tissue - I (680–709)

2012 ICD-9-CM and ICD-10-CM

This section includes infections of the skin and subcutaneous tissue, inflammatory conditions, and other diseases of the skin and subcutaneous tissue.

ICD-10-CM: Diseases of the Skin and Subcutaneous Tissue - L00–L99

Chapter 12 guidelines give directions for coding pressure ulcers. Laterality must now be stated for many conditions, and codes for abscess sites have been expanded. The terms dermatitis and eczema are used interchangeably; be certain your medical record states the cause of the condition before you report any additional codes.

Using the Tabular List only, identify the three-digit category for the following:

		ICD-9-CM	ICD-10-CM
1.	Pressure ulcer	_____	_____
2.	Facial boil	_____	_____
3.	Pemphigus vulgaris	_____	_____
4.	Paronychia of finger	_____	_____
5.	Ingrown nail	_____	_____
6.	Actinic keratosis	_____	_____
7.	Alopecia areata	_____	_____
8.	Cradle cap	_____	_____
9.	Vitiligo	_____	_____
10.	Psoriasis	_____	_____

Name _____

Skin and Subcutaneous Tissue - II (680–709)

Using the alphabetic and/or tabular references, locate the following conditions and code to acceptable specificity, 3 to 7 characters.

		ICD-9-CM	ICD-10-CM
1.	Dermatitis due to alcohol ingestion		
2.	Nail horn, left thumb		
3.	Chronic lichen simplex		
4.	Hives from allergy to trees		
5.	Brocq-Duhring disease		
6.	Erythema multiforme		
7.	Healing pressure ulcer, right elbow		
8.	Cheloid scar		
9.	Furunculosis, left temple		
10.	Asteatosis cutis		
11.	Polymorphous eruption from tanning booth		
12.	Infected corn, right foot		
13.	Lupus erythematosus		
14.	Groin carbuncle, left		
15.	Diaper rash		
16.	Granuloma pyogenicum		
17.	Hutchinson's cheiropompholyx		
18.	Third-degree sunburn		
19.	Gibert's disease		
20.	Angioma serpiginosum		
21.	Impetigination of dermatoses		
22.	Chronic ankle ulcer with muscle necrosis, left		
23.	Dermatitis from contact with gold ring		
24.	Acute cellulitis, right forearm		
25.	Miliaria tropicalis		

Name _____

Musculoskeletal System and Connective Tissue – I (710–739)

2012 ICD-9-CM and ICD-10-CM

This section includes arthropathies and related disorders, dorsopathies, rheumatism (excluding the back), chondropathies, and acquired musculoskeletal deformities. Many codes have a fifth digit. Note that this section excludes fractures.

If you enjoyed coding the musculoskeletal CPT section, you will find this section is even more pleasant. Read very carefully and code only when you are certain of the answer.

Caution: These are large coding lists. You may need information from a previous ICD-9-CM page.

ICD-10-CM: Diseases of the Musculoskeletal System and Connective Tissue - M00–M99

Chapter 13 guidelines clarify site and laterality; acute trauma or chronic/recurrent conditions; pathologic fracture; and osteoporosis. Gout is now included in this chapter. Note that the external cause, if known and documented, is reported after the code for the condition. The "manifestation" codes appearing in italics cannot be reported as a first-listed diagnosis; the underlying disease code must be listed first. This is a large code section and all worksheet items come from the M codes.

Using the Tabular List only, identify the three-digit category for the following:

		ICD-9-CM	ICD-10-CM
1.	Rheumatoid arthritis 714.81	_____	_____
2.	Lumbago	_____	_____
3.	Loose body in right knee	_____	_____
4.	Fibromyositis 729.1	_____	_____
5.	Cauliflower ear	_____	_____
6.	Systemic lupus erythematosus	_____	_____
7.	Polymyalgia rheumatica	_____	_____
8.	Kyphoscoliosis	_____	_____
9.	Kissing spine	_____	_____
10.	Hypertrophic pulmonary osteoarthropathy	_____	_____

Name _____

Musculoskeletal System and Connective Tissue – II (710–739)

Using the alphabetic and/or tabular references, locate the following conditions and code to acceptable specificity, 3 to 7 characters.

		ICD-9-CM	ICD-10-CM
1.	Achilles tenosynovitis, left		
2.	Degenerative osteoarthritis		
3.	Chondromalacia of the left patella		
4.	Tennis elbow, right		
5.	Rhabdomyolysis		
6.	Degenerative arthritis of the lumbar spine		
7.	Staphylococcal pyogenic arthritis		
8.	Cervical radiculopathy		
9.	Old bucket-handle tear, left lateral meniscus		
10.	Swelling in right ankle joint		
11.	Lordosis following laminectomy		
12.	Right plantar fasciitis		
13.	Sjogren's myopathy		
14.	Acute bone infection, right femur		
15.	Calcification of lumbar disc		
16.	Pigeon toes, recent onset		
17.	Torticollis		
18.	Pectus excavatum, acquired		
19.	Postpolio foot drop, left		
20.	Flat feet		
21.	Bowlegs		
22.	Humpback from old age		
23.	Low back pain		
24.	Kashin-Beck disease, right ankle		
25.	Spontaneous left shoulder muscle rupture		

Name _____

Congenital Anomalies - I (740–759)

2012 ICD-9-CM and ICD-10-CM

This section contains conditions that people inherit. These codes differentiate congenital heart disease from acquired heart disease.

ICD-10-CM: Congenital Malformations, Deformations, and Chromosomal Abnormalities - Q00–Q99

Chapter 17 guidelines state that codes from this section can be used throughout the patient's life. However, if the condition has been corrected, use the code indicating a personal history of the condition. Note also that codes from this chapter are not used on maternal or fetal records.

Using the Tabular List only, identify the three-digit category for the following:

		ICD-9-CM	ICD-10-CM
1.	Anophthalmos	_____	_____
2.	Port wine stain	_____	_____
3.	Congenital pectus excavatum	_____	_____
4.	Bicornuate uterus	_____	_____
5.	Missing ear on right	_____	_____
6.	Klinefelter's syndrome	_____	_____
7.	Ventricular septal defect	_____	_____
8.	Cleft lip	_____	_____
9.	Congenital hip deformity	_____	_____
10.	Pyloric stenosis	_____	_____

Name _____

Congenital Anomalies - II (740–759)

Using the alphabetic and/or tabular references, locate the following conditions and code to acceptable specificity, 3 to 7 characters.

		ICD-9-CM	ICD-10-CM
1.	Aphalangia, left foot	_____	_____
2.	Myelomeningocele	_____	_____
3.	Macrodactylism, right thumb	_____	_____
4.	Cauda equina developmental defect	_____	_____
5.	Congenital displacement of the spleen	_____	_____
6.	Cyst of the thyroglossal duct	_____	_____
7.	Newborn glaucoma	_____	_____
8.	True dextrocardia	_____	_____
9.	Postductal coarctation of the aorta	_____	_____
10.	Achondroplastic dwarf	_____	_____
11.	Cryptorchism	_____	_____
12.	Endocardial cushion defect	_____	_____
13.	Middle ear congenital deformity, left	_____	_____
14.	Premature fontanel ossification	_____	_____
15.	Trisomy 21	_____	_____
16.	Autosomal dominant polycystic kidney disease	_____	_____
17.	Congenital heart block	_____	_____
18.	Bloch-Sulzberger melanoblastosis	_____	_____
19.	Congenital polycystic lung disease	_____	_____
20.	Congenital megacolon	_____	_____
21.	Marfan syndrome	_____	_____
22.	Supernumerary first rib	_____	_____
23.	Pseudohermaphroditism	_____	_____
24.	Pes valgus	_____	_____
25.	Cleft nose	_____	_____

Name _____

Conditions of the Perinatal Period - I (760-779)

2012 ICD-9-CM and ICD-10-CM

This unit covers conditions of the perinatal period and may involve both the mother and fetus or infant.

Caution: Item 16 on the next page may be easier to find using the Tabular List.

ICD-10-CM: Certain Conditions Originating in the Perinatal Period - P00–P96

Chapter 16 general guidelines state that these codes relate only to newborn records and are never used on maternal records. Codes include conditions with their origin in the before-birth period through the first 28 days after birth.

There is a mix of maternal and newborn conditions in these worksheets. Does the item describe a condition of the mother or of the fetus? If the mother, use an O code; for the newborn, use a P code.

Note: One code comes from a chapter other than O or P.

The O and P codes may be the most complicated transition from ICD-9-CM to ICD-10-CM.

Using the Tabular List only, identify the three-digit category for the following:

		ICD-9-CM	ICD-10-CM
1.	Maternal malnutrition	_____	_____
2.	Prematurity hyperbilirubinemia	_____	_____
3.	Pregnancy complicated by very large baby	_____	_____
4.	Newborn candidiasis	_____	_____
5.	"Small for dates" newborn	_____	_____
6.	Newborn seizures	_____	_____
7.	Fractured clavicle from birthing	_____	_____
8.	Meconium aspiration	_____	_____
9.	"Infant of diabetic mother" syndrome	_____	_____
10.	Placenta previa	_____	_____

Conditions of the Perinatal Period – II (760–779)

Name _____

Using the alphabetic and/or tabular reference, locate the following conditions and code to acceptable specificity, 3 to 7 characters.

		ICD-9-CM	ICD-10-CM
1.	Umbilical cord thrombosis during delivery	_____	_____
2.	Petechiae of newborn infant	_____	_____
3.	Fetal listeriosis	_____	_____
4.	Delivery by forceps	_____	_____
5.	Newborn transitory tachypnea	_____	_____
6.	Premature delivery of a 730-gm infant	_____	_____
7.	Maternal drug dependence affecting newborn	_____	_____
8.	Facial nerve injury of newborn	_____	_____
9.	Postmature infant	_____	_____
10.	Failure to thrive infant	_____	_____
11.	Hyaline membrane disease	_____	_____
12.	Newborn meconium ileus	_____	_____
13.	Fetal alcohol syndrome	_____	_____
14.	Unstable lie antepartum	_____	_____
15.	ABO erythroblastosis	_____	_____
16.	Fetal chignon from vacuum	_____	_____
17.	Stillborn	_____	_____
18.	Congenital hydrocele	_____	_____
19.	Temporary hypoglycemia of neonate	_____	_____
20.	Hydrops fetalis	_____	_____
21.	Mild newborn asphyxia	_____	_____
22.	Newborn blood loss from cord rupture	_____	_____
23.	Newborn hepatitis	_____	_____
24.	Premature infant anemia	_____	_____
25.	Exchange transfusion thrombocytopenia	_____	_____

Name _____

Symptoms, Signs, and Ill-Defined Conditions – I (780–799)

2012 ICD-9-CM and ICD-10-CM

This section contains codes useful to almost every practice. When you don't know what else to call it, or the record says "rule out," look at coding the symptoms or the signs of the illness or injury that brought the patient to the office.

ICD-10-CM: Symptoms, Signs, and Abnormal Clinical and Laboratory Findings, Not Elsewhere Classified - R00–R99

The general guidelines for Chapter 18 clarify coding symptoms and falls. Codes from this chapter will continue to be very useful in the physician's office. All worksheet items can be found in the R section of ICD-10-CM.

Using the Tabular List only, identify the three-digit category for the following:

		ICD-9-CM	ICD-10-CM
1.	Cardiorespiratory failure	_____	_____
2.	Hoarseness	_____	_____
3.	Anorexia	_____	_____
4.	Old age	_____	_____
5.	Cardiogenic shock	_____	_____
6.	Abnormal EEG	_____	_____
7.	Apnea	_____	_____
8.	Carpopedal spasm	_____	_____
9.	Diarrhea	_____	_____
10.	Colic	_____	_____

Symptoms, Signs, and Ill-Defined Conditions – II (780–799)

Name _____

Using the alphabetic and/or tabular references, locate the following conditions and code to acceptable specificity, 3 to 7 characters.

		ICD-9-CM	ICD-10-CM
1.	Occult blood in feces	_____	_____
2.	Headache	_____	_____
3.	Dysarthria	_____	_____
4.	Epigastric pain	_____	_____
5.	Abdominal distention	_____	_____
6.	Intermittent staggering gait	_____	_____
7.	Chest pain	_____	_____
8.	Enuresis	_____	_____
9.	Acetone in urine	_____	_____
10.	Found dead	_____	_____
11.	Abnormal blushing	_____	_____
12.	Swollen glands	_____	_____
13.	Excessive weight gain	_____	_____
14.	Abnormal weight loss	_____	_____
15.	Positive TB skin test	_____	_____
16.	Nervousness, probable tension	_____	_____
17.	Vertigo	_____	_____
18.	Enlarged spleen	_____	_____
19.	Urinary retention	_____	_____
20.	Coma	_____	_____
21.	Halitosis	_____	_____
22.	Coin lesion, left lung, found on x-ray	_____	_____
23.	All worn out following viral infection	_____	_____
24.	Abnormal liver scan	_____	_____
25.	Dropsy	_____	_____

Name _____

Injury and Poisoning - I (800–999)

2012 ICD-9-CM and ICD-10-CM

This unit contains the diagnoses for fractures, dislocations, sprains, wounds, contusions, burns, poisonings, and other toxic effects and complications. Poisonings are easy to find using the Table of Drugs and Chemicals at the end of the Alphabetic Index.

Caution: Watch out (again) for the codes requiring a fifth digit. Also, what kind of injury would result from the incident in item 12 on the next page? Search on that term.

ICD-10-CM: Injury, Poisoning, and Certain Other Consequences of External Causes - S00–T88

Chapter 19 guidelines explain coding for injuries, burns, and adverse effects. Review them carefully. Note that the S codes relate to different types of injuries to a single body region; the T codes cover injuries to unspecified body regions as well as poisoning and certain other consequences of external causes. This section has some large tables for the 7th character (see S72) and will require careful documentation in the medical record. You may use a second code from the next chapter, "External Causes of Morbidity" (V00–Y99), if the medical record documents the cause of the injury. Codes in the T section may include the external cause.

There are many placeholder x's in these codes; one item requires two codes.

Using the Tabular List only, identify the three-digit category for the following:

		ICD-9-CM	ICD-10-CM
1.	Accidental Penicillin poisoning	_____	_____
2.	Anaphylactic shock	_____	_____
3.	Wrist sprain, left	_____	_____
4.	Frostbite, mild, left ear	_____	_____
5.	Fracture of temporal bone	_____	_____
6.	Open wound of toe	_____	_____
7.	Mechanical complication of dialysis catheter	_____	_____
8.	Burn of fingers	_____	_____
9.	Right nursemaids elbow	_____	_____
10.	Heel blister	_____	_____

Name _____

Injury and Poisoning - II (800–999)

Using the alphabetic and/or tabular references, locate the following conditions and code to acceptable specificity, 3 to 7 characters.

		ICD-9-CM	ICD-10-CM
1.	Late effect of air embolus following transfusion	_____	_____
2.	Recent C5–C7 cord injury with complete lesion	_____	_____
3.	Second visit for open wound of scalp	_____	_____
4.	Visit for sequelae of concussion (48-hour coma) now recovered	_____	_____
5.	Dislocation, right acromioclavicular joint, 2 hours ago	_____	_____
6.	Sunstroke earlier today	_____	_____
7.	History of battered spouse syndrome	_____	_____
8.	Four-inch laceration with embedded gravel, left lower arm	_____	_____
9.	Accidental poisoning by wild mushrooms	_____	_____
10.	Peritonitis due to retained surgical sponge	_____	_____
11.	Third-degree burn, right upper back	_____	_____
12.	Dropped heavy trunk on left great toe	_____	_____
13.	Fifteen infected mosquito bites, lower leg	_____	_____
14.	Struck by lightning 6 months ago while golfing	_____	_____
15.	Open fracture of left metatarsal bones	_____	_____
16.	Rejection of kidney transplant	_____	_____
17.	Leaking silicone breast implant	_____	_____
18.	Follow-up visit for abrasion, left lower leg	_____	_____
19.	Colles' fracture, right	_____	_____
20.	Drank rubbing alcohol	_____	_____
21.	Delayed healing, fracture of the sternum	_____	_____
22.	Esophageal burns, drank "Easy-Off" oven cleaner	_____	_____
23.	Sprained ankle	_____	_____
24.	Pneumothorax from stab wound to chest	_____	_____
25.	Removed 3 small stones from left ear canal	_____	_____

Supplementary Classification - "V" Codes- I (V01–V91)

2012 ICD-9-CM and ICD-10-CM

These codes are used as a "diagnosis" for a person who: (a) is receiving services for a specific purpose but is not currently sick, such as vaccination; (b) seeks treatment for a specific disorder such as chemotherapy; or (c) has some circumstance or problem present that influences the patient's health status but is not itself a current illness or injury, such as a history of cancer. Insurers may not pay for some of these codes, as they may question the medical necessity of treatment for well persons. Many managed care plans providing preventive care expect the office to use these codes when the patient is seen for routine care.

Caution: Some terms are not easy to find in the Alphabetic Index.

ICD-10-CM: Factors Influencing Health Status and Contact with Health Services - Z00–Z99

Chapter 21 guidelines state they can be used in any health care setting but only certain Z codes may be the first-listed diagnosis codes. The familiar V codes have become Z codes. The Z codes are used when circumstances other than a disease, an injury, or an external cause are recorded as problems or as the diagnosis. Note that abnormal findings disclosed at the time of these examinations are classified as R codes. These Z codes include the routine examination and screening services.

Note: One code comes from another chapter

Using the Tabular List only, identify the V and two-digit category for the following:

		ICD-9-CM	ICD-10-CM
1.	Twenty-two-year-old male with BMI of 32.7	_____	_____
2.	Artificial eye fitting	_____	_____
3.	Family planning	_____	_____
4.	TIA episode last year	_____	_____
5.	Triplets, born at home	_____	_____
6.	Seen for ear piercing	_____	_____
7.	MMR immunization	_____	_____
8.	Mother died of breast CA	_____	_____
9.	Exposure to rubella	_____	_____
10.	Patient "worried well"	_____	_____

Name _____

Supplementary Classification - "V" Codes – II (V01–V91)

Using the alphabetic and/or tabular references, locate the following conditions and code to acceptable specificity, 3 to 7 characters.

		ICD-9-CM	ICD-10-CM
1.	Counseling, contraceptive foam use	_____	_____
2.	Camp physical exam	_____	_____
3.	Twin delivery, 1 stillborn	_____	_____
4.	Male, family history of kidney CA	_____	_____
5.	Adult, was battered as a child	_____	_____
6.	Drug allergy by history	_____	_____
7.	Living cornea donor	_____	_____
8.	Going to India, needs cholera vaccine	_____	_____
9.	Routine check for status of cystostomy	_____	_____
10.	Spent night with syphilitic partner	_____	_____
11.	Refused vaccine based on religion	_____	_____
12.	Viral hepatitis carrier	_____	_____
13.	Has lymphocytic leukemia	_____	_____
14.	Treated for alcoholism, 1986	_____	_____
15.	Routine chest x-ray, food handler	_____	_____
16.	Problems with mother-in-law	_____	_____
17.	Orthodontia appliance adjusted	_____	_____
18.	Receiving estrogen, postmenopausal	_____	_____
19.	Annual gyn exam	_____	_____
20.	Respirator dependent	_____	_____
21.	Recently in India, worried about exposure to cholera	_____	_____
22.	Allergy testing	_____	_____
23.	Supervision/examination for week-old infant	_____	_____
24.	Screening for sickle-cell disorder	_____	_____
25.	Has artificial heart implant	_____	_____

Supplementary Classification - "E" Codes- I (E000–E999)

2012 ICD-9-CM and ICD-10-CM

These codes describe the external causes of injury or poisoning. They are used in addition to the actual condition treated. If you set a fractured femur caused by an automobile accident, code the fracture first (primary) and the E code second. The use of the E code could indicate that the primary responsibility for payment rests with some other agency besides the health insurance carrier, such as a taxicab company or the railroad.

Caution: Read the instructions carefully before beginning the coding exercises. Note that the reference to the fourth digit results in a five-character code.

ICD-10-CM: External Causes of Morbidity - V00–Y99

Chapter 20 guidelines state that these codes are secondary for use in any health care setting. They now include information on coding injuries from terrorism, suspected terrorism, and the secondary effects of terrorism.

The familiar E codes of these worksheets will have codes from T, V, W, X, and even a code from the H section. Use the index to make it easier to find the correct code.

Using the Tabular List only (if possible), identify the E and three-digit category for the following:

		ICD-9-CM	ICD-10-CM
1.	Injured when train collided with downed tree	_____	_____
2.	Wood alcohol poisoning	_____	_____
3.	Fell from ski-lift gondola	_____	_____
4.	Smoker injured when bed set on fire	_____	_____
5.	Accidental aspirin poisoning	_____	_____
6.	Fell out of bed	_____	_____
7.	Bitten by a shark	_____	_____
8.	Accidentally pushed from moving car	_____	_____
9.	Trampled by crowd in a panic	_____	_____
10.	Wrong procedure, right patient	_____	_____

Name _____

Supplementary Classification – "E" Codes – II (E800–E999)

Using the alphabetic and/or tabular references, locate the following conditions and code to acceptable specificity, 3 to 7 characters. You might find the Index to External Causes helpful.

		ICD-9-CM	ICD-10-CM
1.	Accidentally got a sea anemone sting	_____	_____
2.	Passenger hurt when snowmobile hit tree	_____	_____
3.	Killed by handgun, possible homicide	_____	_____
4.	Bicyclist collided with train	_____	_____
5.	Bicyclist collided with wall	_____	_____
6.	Slashed wrists in suicide attempt	_____	_____
7.	Loss of hearing from rock music	_____	_____
8.	Injured during earthquake	_____	_____
9.	Diving accident, hit bottom of pool	_____	_____
10.	Hurt at camp site, minivan steps collapsed	_____	_____
11.	Thrown from horse and buggy in collision with car	_____	_____
12.	Pilot injured when hot air balloon crashed	_____	_____
13.	Four-year-old drank gasoline from pop bottle	_____	_____
14.	Injured by fireworks	_____	_____
15.	Overcome by Agent Orange in Vietnam	_____	_____
16.	Failure of aortic valve prosthesis, 4 days postop	_____	_____
17.	Severe reaction, used prescribed dose of eye meds	_____	_____
18.	Burned while tending fireplace at cottage	_____	_____
19.	Dehydration, water to home turned off	_____	_____
20.	Human bites, left arm, 3-year-old male	_____	_____
21.	Almost drowned when washed overboard during storm	_____	_____
22.	Infection, contaminated during heart cath	_____	_____
23.	Hand slashed by circular saw	_____	_____
24.	Accidental ether poisoning at fraternity party	_____	_____
25.	Skin frozen, contact with dry ice	_____	_____

Name _____

PUTTING IT ALL TOGETHER

This series of case studies asks you to find the correct procedure and diagnosis codes. Note also that you are asked to include any required modifier. The answers and the rationale for the answer follow this section. Read the case studies carefully, look for key terms, and be certain to follow all coding rules from CPT, ICD-9-CM, and ICD-10-CM.

1. The patient had a moderately progressive left keratoconus and no longer has adequate functional vision. To delay the need for corneal transplant, Dr. Light scheduled the patient for intrastromal corneal ring segmental implants.

    Proc/Mod _____ ICD-9-CM _____ ICD-10-CM _____
    _____   _____   _____
    _____   _____   _____
    _____   _____   _____

2. A 22-year-old male was admitted to a residential psychiatric facility for treatment of an exacerbation of Asperger's syndrome. Following a comprehensive workup, he had 25 minutes of biofeedback psychotherapy on the day of admission.

    Proc/Mod _____ ICD-9-CM _____ ICD-10-CM _____
    _____   _____   _____
    _____   _____   _____
    _____   _____   _____

3. In June, Dr. Walton spent 35 minutes supervising and coordinating the care of his patient, 83-year-old John Roberts. John left the nursing home and moved into assisted living at the Maple Senior Center where he will be under the care of Maple Home Services. Mr. Roberts had recovered sufficiently from his left-sided paralysis following a stroke, and, since he was right-handed, he could now feed and dress himself. Mr. Roberts had a mild monoplegia of the left lower leg so Dr. Walton provided him with a folding wheeled walker for ambulation.

    Proc/Mod _____ ICD-9-CM _____ ICD-10-CM _____
    _____   _____   _____
    _____   _____   _____
    _____   _____   _____

Name _____

4. Dr. Jack Armstrong, a rehabilitation specialist, discharged Mary Martin from City Hospital following surgery to repair a pathologic fracture of the right hip. The same day, the doctor admitted her to the Meadows Continuing Care facility for physical therapy and long-term care.

   Proc/Mod _____   ICD-9-CM _____   ICD-10-CM _____
   _____   _____   _____
   _____   _____   _____
   _____   _____   _____

5. Michael Jaydan injured his left thumb playing basketball. He was seen in Dr. Spaulding's after hours urgent care center. The doctor performed a new patient EPF visit and took two x-rays of the left thumb. There was no fracture. Dr. Spaulding treated the sprain injury by strapping the thumb with a 3-inch elastic compression bandage.

   Proc/Mod _____   ICD-9-CM _____   ICD-10-CM _____
   _____   _____   _____
   _____   _____   _____
   _____   _____   _____

6. Paul Brown, age 87, was scheduled at Metropolitan Hospital for outpatient surgery to replace his mature right cataract with a lens implant. Just as Dr. Black was to begin the procedure, Mr. Brown developed a significant cardiac dysrhythmia. The surgery was canceled and Dr. Black admitted Mr. Brown to the hospital's observation unit for care of the arrhythmia. Dr. Green, a cardiologist, later that day admitted Mr. Brown to Metropolitan Hospital for a complete cardiac workup.

   Code the services of Dr. Black.

   Proc/Mod _____   ICD-9-CM _____   ICD-10-CM _____
   _____   _____   _____
   _____   _____   _____
   _____   _____   _____

7. An ambulance brought a 37-year-old man to the Central City Hospital ER after he was injured in a hit-and-run accident. The orthopedic surgeon, Dr. Frost, treated the patient in the emergency department for a fractured distal phalanx, right ring finger; a fractured mandible on the right; and the closed treatment of a fractured right femur shaft. When the patient was stable, Dr. Robins admitted him to Central City Hospital for continuing care of the fractures. Code Dr. Frost's services.

   Proc/Mod _____   ICD-9-CM _____   ICD-10-CM _____
   _____   _____   _____
   _____   _____   _____
   _____   _____   _____

Name _____

8. Dr. Dallas discharged 79-year-old Mary Stuart from Mercy Medical Center after she recovered from an extrinsic status asthmaticus attack. She was seen that afternoon in his office for wheezing that did not respond to a non-compounded 1-mg unit-dose albuterol nebulizer treatment. She was readmitted to Mercy for further care of her acute asthma episode.

Proc/Mod _____   ICD-9-CM _____   ICD-10-CM _____

_____   _____   _____

_____   _____   _____

_____   _____   _____

9. Jennifer Taylor, age 4, was seen by her osteopathic pediatrician after she had been ill for two days with a productive cough and now had developed a fever. Her examination focused on the presenting problems. The doctor diagnosed bronchitis and a somatic dysfunction of the cervical, thoracic, rib, and abdominal areas. She was treated with medication and OMT.

Proc/Mod _____   ICD-9-CM _____   ICD-10-CM _____

_____   _____   _____

_____   _____   _____

_____   _____   _____

10. Harry Morgan, who has Type 2 diabetes and severe osteoarthritis, was seen to discuss his recent lab work. When he appeared uncoordinated and confused, Dr. Jessup did a glucose test with a reagent strip that showed Mr. Morgan's glucose level was low. Mr. Morgan was given crackers and a drink and later retested. Dr. Jessup became concerned that Harry was not taking his medications correctly or perhaps had developed a new problem, so he ordered a comprehensive metabolic panel. Mr. Morgan was in the office for over an hour and monitored closely by the doctor.

Proc/Mod _____   ICD-9-CM _____   ICD-10-CM _____

_____   _____   _____

_____   _____   _____

_____   _____   _____

Name _____

11. When Dr. Davis saw Ralph Cramer in a subsequent inpatient visit today, the patient stated he wanted to get out of the hospital in time for his granddaughter's birthday party tomorrow. His only complaints were some backache from spending a week in a hospital bed. The doctor ordered a final lab test to confirm that the severe urinary tract infection that required the hospitalization was no longer present. Dr. Davis told Mr. Cramer he would return by noon tomorrow and, if the lab work showed no problems, he would send him home at that time.

   Proc/Mod _____   ICD-9-CM _____   ICD-10-CM _____
   _____   _____   _____
   _____   _____   _____
   _____   _____   _____

12. Fred Smith returned to his cardiologist's office for a six-month recheck of the medications for his hypertensive heart disease. His EKG showed abnormalities, so Dr. Peck ordered a cardiovascular stress test to be done before Mr. Smith left the office. The doctor's physician assistant supervised the test and prepared the tracing for Dr. Peck's interpretation. The stress test revealed ischemia, possibly related to a recent "silent" myocardial infarction. Mr. Smith was scheduled for further workup.

   Proc/Mod _____   ICD-9-CM _____   ICD-10-CM _____
   _____   _____   _____
   _____   _____   _____
   _____   _____   _____

13. A male patient was seen in his family doctor's office as an emergency. He was treated with an insect venom injection for anaphylaxis, secondary to a bee sting.

   Proc/Mod _____   ICD-9-CM _____   ICD-10-CM _____
   _____   _____   _____
   _____   _____   _____
   _____   _____   _____

Name _____

14. A 19-year-old male took his girlfriend hunting. Her shotgun accidentally discharged in the duck blind and he was hit just below the right eye by a ricocheted shot. He had no change in vision but did have a small laceration and bruising in the area. Films in the emergency department revealed a metal foreign body embedded in the right eyelid, just above the laceration. The cheek laceration was sutured and the foreign body removed by the ER physician. The patient was advised to see his primary care physician for follow-up care. The gunshot accident was reported to the authorities. The foreign body was given to the patient, who wanted it as a "souvenir."

Proc/Mod _____ ICD-9-CM _____ ICD-10-CM _____
_____ _____ _____
_____ _____ _____
_____ _____ _____

15. A 37-year-old new patient was seen in the office for trauma to the left elbow received in a fall. Two x-rays of the elbow revealed no fracture. The patient was advised to rest the arm and use hot or cold compresses on the swelling, depending on which made it feel better. He was asked to contact the office if the arm was not better in days. As the patient was about to leave the exam room, he asked the doctor to remove the cerumen from both ears. This was done with a curette and lavage.

Proc/Mod _____ ICD-9-CM _____ ICD-10-CM _____
_____ _____ _____
_____ _____ _____
_____ _____ _____

16. Dr. Brady, a pediatrician in solo practice, performed a routine newborn exam on Baby Boy Peterson. Later that day the baby developed a severe, but not critical, respiratory distress and was transferred to the care of Dr. Lewis, a neonatologist, who admitted the baby to the neonatal intensive care unit (NICU).

Dr. Brady's
Proc/Mod _____ ICD-9-CM _____ ICD-10-CM _____
_____ _____ _____

Dr. Lewis's
Proc/Mod _____ ICD-9-CM _____ ICD-10-CM _____
_____ _____ _____

Name _____

17. The client was seen in a full 50-minute session psychotherapy visit for a posttraumatic stress disorder. Dr. Bauer asked her to stay longer for biofeedback training to help her stop smoking and reduce stress.

Proc/Mod _____   ICD-9-CM _____   ICD-10-CM _____

_____   _____   _____

_____   _____   _____

_____   _____   _____

18. Dr. Franklin left a group practice in East Jordan and set up private practice in Summerville, a town about 25 miles west of East Jordan. Some of her patients followed her to the new practice. She set up new records for these patients and incorporated copies of the group practice records in these charts. She saw Robert Taylor from her prior practice for an expanded problem focused visit and for the six-month renewal of his prescriptions for Type 2 diabetes.

Proc/Mod _____   ICD-9-CM _____   ICD-10-CM _____

_____   _____   _____

_____   _____   _____

_____   _____   _____

19. The 13-year-old patient had an abscess on the right middle finger and a sebaceous cyst of the left first toe. Both lesions were treated by I&D at the same operative session.

Proc/Mod _____   ICD-9-CM _____   ICD-10-CM _____

_____   _____   _____

_____   _____   _____

_____   _____   _____

20. John Williams, a 59-year-old real estate agent, complained of occasional rectal bleeding over the past year. He was scheduled for a diagnostic flexible sigmoidoscopy. The surgeon also removed three polyps using bipolar cautery. Two polyps were removed intact while the third polyp had to be removed piecemeal. All lesions were proximal to the splenic flexure.

Proc/Mod _____   ICD-9-CM _____   ICD-10-CM _____

_____   _____   _____

_____   _____   _____

_____   _____   _____

Name _____

21. Frank Johnson had worsening pain in his right knee over the past year. Dr. Butler performed a diagnostic arthroscopy that included a partial medial meniscectomy and chondroplasty of two compartments of the right knee.

   Proc/Mod _____   ICD-9-CM _____   ICD-10-CM _____

   _____   _____   _____
   _____   _____   _____
   _____   _____   _____

22. The emergency room doctor at City Hospital diagnosed a 19-week missed abortion for Martha Thomas. She was treated with prostaglandin and subsequently delivered all the products of conception.

   Proc/Mod _____   ICD-9-CM _____   ICD-10-CM _____

   _____   _____   _____
   _____   _____   _____
   _____   _____   _____

23. George Smith had not seen Dr. Mann for two years when he returned to the office concerned about some "red bumps" on his face, neck, and arms. After an EPF visit to Dr. Mann who diagnosed the "bumps" as actinic keratoses, the doctor removed a skin tag from the neck/shoulder area where it had been irritated by Mr. Smith's shirt collars.

   Proc/Mod _____   ICD-9-CM _____   ICD-10-CM _____

   _____   _____   _____
   _____   _____   _____
   _____   _____   _____

24. Phyllis Young had been hospitalized for a day when her doctor asked Dr. Samuel Sterns, a surgeon, to see her for abdominal pain. Dr. Sterns examined her and diagnosed gallstones. He scheduled Ms. Young for a laparoscopic cholecystectomy later that day.

   Proc/Mod _____   ICD-9-CM _____   ICD-10-CM _____

   _____   _____   _____
   _____   _____   _____
   _____   _____   _____

Name _____

25. A mother brought her 6-month-old infant to the office for a split virus flu immunization and was seen by the nurse. The nurse reviewed the vaccine information sheet with the mother and gave her a copy of the document. The mother stated that she noticed that her son had a cough but there had been no change in his behavior and he did not act as though he were ill. He had no fever. The nurse checked and documented the child's vital signs, and noted that there were no contraindications to administering the vaccine at today's visit.

Proc/Mod _____   ICD-9-CM _____   ICD-10-CM _____
           _____   _____   _____
           _____   _____   _____
           _____   _____   _____

Putting It All Together—Answers and Rationales

1. Proc/Mod: 0099T   Diagnosis: 371.60 H18.602

   The procedure appears in CPT as a Category III Code. Keratoconus is listed as stable (a slow, persistent worsening), acute (sudden, severe onset), or unstable. Since a "moderately progressive" disease state is not in the list, code the diagnosis as unspecified.

2. Proc/Mod: 99305, 90875   Diagnosis: 299.80 F84.5

   CPT states that medical psychotherapy is reported in addition to the E/M service.

3. Proc/Mod: 99316, E0143   Diagnosis: 438.22, 438.42   I69.354, I69.844

   There was medical treatment at the nursing facility and the time exceeded 30 minutes. The service would be a discharge of more than 30 minutes from a nursing facility rather than the care plan oversight service. Providing the walker is code E0143. The diagnoses must relate to late effects of a stroke (438.xx), not on the acute event. Note how the late effect of cerebrovascular disease (438) is focused on the sequelae following the causal event.

4. Proc/Mod: 99238, 99304   Diagnosis: 733.14 S72.001A

   Because two facilities are involved, the discharge from the acute care hospital and the admission to the nursing facility may both be reported. Since the patient's condition is familiar to the doctor, it is unlikely that the discharge would exceed 30 minutes and the nursing facility admission reflects the moderate severity of the patient's condition. Caution: Some payers may not allow the same physician to report services in two medical facilities on the same day.

5. Proc/Mod: 90202-25, 73120-LT, 29280-FA, A6449   Diagnosis: 842.10   S63.682A

   The modifier –25 would allow payment of the new patient office visit when a treatment is performed at the same visit. When reporting strapping, remember to include the required supplies. A fracture was not confirmed. Note that "sprain, thumb" refers to 842.10, a sprain of "unspecified site" of the hand even though the site was identified (ICD-9-CM), while ICD-10-CM has codes for the thumb.

6. Proc/Mod: 99235   Diagnosis: 366.17, 427.9 H25.9, I49.9

   Procedure code 99235, rather than 99219, is correct because Dr. Black admitted and discharged (by a transfer of care) Mr. Brown on the same day. Dr. Green will report the initial hospital care service, 99221–99223. The diagnosis codes for Dr. Black would be the cataract first and arrhythmia second. "When a patient presents for outpatient surgery and develops complications requiring admission to observation, code the reason for the surgery as the first reported diagnosis (reason for the encounter), followed by codes for the complications as secondary diagnoses." (Guidelines, A 2)

7. Proc/Mod: 27502, 21450-51-RT, 26600-51-F8   Diagnosis: 821.01, 802.20, 816.00

    S72.301A, S02.609A, S62.634A

   Remember to put the most significant surgery on the first line, regardless of how they are listed on the operative note. Since the descriptions did not refer to a manipulation, use codes that state "no manipulation." Modifier –51 is required on the 2nd and 3rd services, as well as the modifier describing the finger. Mandible diagnosis code will be "unspecified" since the part was not identified; the distal phalanx and the shaft of the femur are identified and coded by site.

8. Proc/Mod: 99238, 94640, J7613, 99221-25   Diagnosis: 493.01, 786.07, 493.92

    J45.902, R06.2, J45.901

   This is an example of claims you will need to monitor. There are three claims: one for each hospitalization and one for the office services. The office visit is not billed, as those services are related to the hospital admission of the same day. Modifier –25 is required for the admission, as it is not related to the other E/M service (discharge) reported that day. The diagnosis for the discharge service, 493.01, describes the findings of her hospital stay. The diagnosis for the office services would be the symptom, wheezing, 786.07; the diagnosis for admission, 493.92, asthma, with acute exacerbation. Be prepared to fight for payment on this one.

9. Proc/Mod: 99212-25, 98926   Diagnosis: 490, 739.9   J40, M99.09

   Use modifier –25 on the office visit to indicate that the diagnosis was made today. Do not count on the fact there are two diagnoses to explain that the services are not related. Note the body regions identified in the CPT OMT codes. The diagnosis 490, bronchitis, is not specified as acute or chronic. The somatic dysfunction codes would be 739.0-9. Since 739.9 states abdomen and other, it is the diagnosis code for the OMT service.

10. Proc/Mod: 99215, 82948, 82948-91   Diagnosis: 250.00 E11.69, R41.0, R27.8

    The extended office visit is based on time, not the level of the examination. The repeat lab test needs the –91 modifier. The metabolic panel was ordered, not performed in the office. The severe osteoarthritis did not impact today's visit so that diagnosis is not reported. ICD-10-CM code E11.69 states "Use additional code to identify complication." The record includes "uncoordinated and confused" so those codes are also reported.

11. Proc/Mod: 99231   Diagnosis: 724.5, 599.0   M54.9, N39.0

    A higher level of inpatient visit would be incorrect. The patient is stable today if he is to be discharged tomorrow. Today's complaint, backache, would be the diagnosis for this visit and the urinary tract infection would be reported as the diagnosis for the lab work ordered.

12. Proc/Mod: 99213-25, 93000-59, 93015   Diagnosis: 402.90, 794.31   I11.9, R94.31

    The office visit is likely to be an expanded problem-focused visit, with –25 to indicate the visit should not be included in the diagnostic tests. The 12-lead EKG could require the modifier –51 or –59 or payers might bundle it in with the stress test. The diagnosis 402.90 would be used for the office visit and the EKG, while the best diagnosis for the stress test is the abnormal EKG code, 794.31. Avoid the diagnosis "ischemia," as the cause has not been determined and cannot be labeled chronic based on this information.

13. Proc/Mod: 99215-25, 95130   Diagnosis: 995.0, 989.5, E905.3   T63.441

    This is a problem of high severity. Modifier –25 should be used to indicate the office visit was separate from the injection. Use 995.0 for the office visit, and 989.5 (toxic effect of venom) for the injection. Reporting E905.3 may be optional. Note that the ICD-10-CM code assumes the sting was unintentional as most people who are allergic to bees avoid them. One ICD-10-CM code would probably be adequate for both services.

14. Proc/Mod: 67938-54, 12011-54-51   Diagnosis: 930.8, 873.41, E922.1

                                                                                                           S01.411A, S01.121A, W33.01xA

    Since the removal of an embedded foreign body is the major procedure, it should be reported first. Use modifier –54 on both procedures to indicate the services are surgical care only. The services relate to only one area of the body, so there probably would be no E/M service. Use diagnosis code 930.8 rather than 930.9, as the site is specified, but not as conjunctival sac (930.1) or the lacrimal punctum (930.2). If the documentation supported an E/M service, such as abrasions from other pieces of shot, it would be 99281-25, indicating it is unrelated to the surgical service. The gunshot accident code, E922.1, may be optional.

15. Proc/Mod: 99201-25, 73070-LT, 69210   Diagnosis: 923.11, 380.4   S50.02xA, H61.23

    The examination was focused on the elbow and requires modifier –25, separate from the surgical service, 69210. Use modifier –LT on the x-ray. Get into the habit of using right and left indicators as laterality is significant in ICD-10-CM. Since there was no fracture or open wound, the diagnosis must be contusion for the first two services. Use impacted cerumen, 380.4 (H61.23), for the 69210.

16. Dr. Brady's Proc/Mod: 99460   Diagnosis: V20.31 Z00.110

    Dr. Lewis's Proc/Mod: 99223   Diagnosis: 770.89 P22.9

    Dr. Brady's service was the newborn exam and is billable since he is not in practice with the neonatologist. The diagnosis, at the time of his visit, would have been a normal newborn. The problem occurred later. This was not stated as a "critical" admission, so the regular initial care services would be reported, but it would be reasonable to report a high level of service. Note the infant age range in both ICD-9-CM and ICD-10-CM. The "respiratory distress" should be coded in general terms only since it was not described as a syndrome.

17. Proc/Mod: 90806, 90901-51   Diagnosis: 309.81, 305.11   F43.10, F17.210

    Use the two codes rather than 90876, which combines the two services into one code as they did not occur concurrently. Modifier –51 or –59 clarifies two separate services. The diagnosis could be reported as PTSD (309.81) for both services, or tobacco abuse (305.11) for the biofeedback. Avoid using codes from psychological trauma (V15.41, V15.42) or psychosocial circumstances (V62.89). For mental health services, it is advisable to code on the "light" side. Reveal no more than necessary to get the claim paid.

18. Proc/Mod: 99213   Diagnosis: 250.00 E11.9

    Assuming that she was the doctor who prescribed the meds six months ago, this would be an established patient visit. If Mr. Taylor is transferring to her practice and has had no professional services in the past three years from Dr. Franklin or another physician of the same specialty in her former practice, this would be a new patient visit, 99202. The change in tax identification numbers and establishing a new chart does not make this a new patient visit. E11.9 will probably be one of the most used codes in ICD-10-CM.

19. Proc/Mod: 10061-F7-TA   Diagnosis: 681.00, 706.2   L02.511, L72.1

Do not report two codes, 10060-F7 and 10060-TA, as the description for 10061 states "multiple." Code 10061 would be the correct procedure code even though the treatment areas are separate. Report both diagnoses; the order of the diagnosis codes would not matter. Using both modifiers and two diagnosis codes may result in an adequate payment, but if it doesn't, it could help with the appeal.

20. Proc/Mod: 45333   Diagnosis: 211.3 D12.6

CPT states: "surgical endoscopy always includes diagnostic endoscopy." Code 45333 is used once, regardless of the number of polyps removed. Also, it makes no difference if the polyp is removed whole or in pieces. The diagnosis should be polyp of the colon, rather than rectal bleeding. As there is no mention of malignancy, be certain you select diagnosis codes from the benign section.

21. Proc/Mod: 29881-RT, G0289-51-RT   Diagnosis: 717.82, 717.7   M23.231, M94.261

The arthroscopic meniscectomy with chondroplasty is the major procedure and should be reported first. CMS created G0289, for reporting chondroplasty on a separate compartment. Modifier –51 would be reported first as it is a pricing modifier; modifier –RT explains that only the right knee was involved in the surgery. If you work for an orthopedic surgeon, contact the payers to determine if they will accept and pay for the G-code and if they allow it to be reported with a quantity of more than 1. A torn meniscus could be a current or an old injury. Report the old injury, 717.82 (M23.231), for the first service, and chondromalacia, 717.7 (M94.261), for the other service.

22. Proc/Mod: 59855   Diagnosis: 632& O02.1

Note that the procedure code includes all the visits associated with the abortion service. The diagnosis is one of the few three-digit codes in the section on pregnancy and childbirth.

23. Proc/Mod: 99213-25, 11200   Diagnosis: 702.0& L57.0, 701.9& L91.8

The visit was more complex than the usual preoperative evaluation and postoperative care for a single skin tag with the finding of actinic keratoses. Modifier –25 is required for the office visit, as the 99213 was when the irritated skin tag was found. Use codes 702.0 (L54.0) for the office visit, and 701.9 (L91.8) for the surgical service.

24. Proc/Mod: 99252-57, 47562   Diagnosis: 789.00, 574.20   R10.9, K80.20

Dr. Sterns's first visit with the patient was the consultation, and the –57 indicates that the decision for surgery was made then. However, if this lady has Medicare, CMS states this is not a consultation but should be reported as an initial or subsequent visit. Since the admitting physician (the primary care doctor) reported the initial day of inpatient care (yesterday), Dr. Sterns would report a subsequent hospital visit, 99231 or 99232, with the modifier –57. If this Medicare rule becomes part of a future CPT, this rule would apply to all payers.

25. Proc/Mod: 99211-25, 90657, 90471   Diagnosis:786.2, V04.81   R05, Z23

This is a good example of the proper use of code 99211 and the "cough" diagnosis for the visit. Had the child been examined yesterday and returned today for the immunization, you would report only the immunization (90657) and the administration service (90471).

EXAM QUESTIONS FOR CPT, CPT AND HCPCS, AND ICD-9-CM

Directions:

- Use the appropriate coding manual to determine the correct choice for each situation.
- Answer sheet is provided at the end of each exam for recording your choice for each question.

Name _____

Exam Questions for CPT

Directions: Use the appropriate coding manual to determine the correct choice for each situation.

1. Patient underwent nerve grafting of the right foot, 3 cm.
   ① 64885-RT
   ② 64890-RT
   ③ 64891-RT
   ④ 64901-RT

2. Patient underwent thyroidectomy for removal of remaining thyroid tissue after previous right lobectomy for suspected malignancy.
   ① 60225
   ② 60240
   ③ 60260
   ④ 60270

3. Established patient, a nursing facility resident, was seen for annual assessment.
   ① 99201
   ② 99310
   ③ 99318
   ④ 99336

4. An 81-year-old patient receives anesthesia prior to undergoing cardioversion for persistent infrequent arrhythmia. Include physical status modifier with code.
   ① 00400-P2 + 99100
   ② 00410-P3
   ③ 00410-P2 + 99100
   ④ 00410-P4

5. Surgeon performs a sphenoid sinusotomy for removal of polyps, including biopsy.
   ① 31020
   ② 31050
   ③ 31051
   ④ 31070

6. Physician performs a surgical biopsy of the right temporal artery.
   ① 37200
   ② 37605
   ③ 37609
   ④ 37799

7. A 67-year-old patient underwent contact laser vaporization of the prostate.
   ① 52450
   ② 52601
   ③ 52647
   ④ 52648

8. Patient underwent total abdominal hysterectomy, sparing the tubes and ovaries.
   ① 58150
   ② 58152
   ③ 58200
   ④ 58210

9. Radiologist directs and interprets the placement of a long gastrostomy tube in a patient who is status post cerebrovascular accident.
   ① 43246-26
   ② 74340
   ③ 74355
   ④ 74363

10. Nursing home patient was admitted for management of pneumonia which is now resolved. The physician came by the facility to discharge the patient to home, spending 20 minutes with the patient and family.
    ① 99217
    ② 99238
    ③ 99315
    ④ 99339

11. The physician conducted an initial office consultation for a 44-year-old patient, six years status post lumbar laminectomy, with intractable sciatic pain, depression, and history of narcotic dependency/abuse, high complexity.

    ① 99241
    ② 99243
    ③ 99244
    ④ 99245

12. A 16-year-old patient undergoes excision of an aneurysmal bone cyst of the proximal right humerus, with allograft.

    ① 23155
    ② 23156
    ③ 23184
    ④ 23220

13. A 15-year-old otherwise healthy patient receives anesthesia for electroconvulsive therapy. Include physical status modifier with code.

    ① 00104-P1
    ② 00104-P2
    ③ 00190-P1
    ④ 00210-P1

14. Patient who is status post cochlear implant has visit for group rehabilitation, treatment of speech, and a processing disorder.

    ① 92506
    ② 92508
    ③ 92520
    ④ 92557

15. Healthcare employee receives the first of three Hepatitis B vaccinations IM from her doctor.

    ① 90371 + 96372
    ② 90746 + 90471
    ③ 90746 + 96372
    ④ 96372

16. Patient underwent cervical conization with loop electrical excision of the transitional zone.

    ① 57460
    ② 57500
    ③ 57520
    ④ 57522

17. Patient underwent stereotactic biopsy of intracranial lesion under MR guidance.

    ① 61720
    ② 61750
    ③ 61751
    ④ 61770

18. Dr. Harris counsels a group of teenagers regarding sexually transmitted diseases and prevention. Session lasts 30 minutes.

    ① 99401
    ② 99402
    ③ 99411
    ④ 99411-26

19. Dr. Nuri examines an 18-year-old in the emergency department for recurrent, severe menstrual migraine headache.

    ① 99241
    ② 99281
    ③ 99282
    ④ 99284

20. Patient underwent in-office simple incision and drainage of a pilonidal cyst.

    ① 10060
    ② 10061
    ③ 10080
    ④ 10081

21. Surgeon removes a Harrington rod in a patient with chronic irritation in the region of insertion.

    ① 22849
    ② 22850
    ③ 22852
    ④ 22899

22. Patient with congenital cleft palate underwent rhinoplasty with columellar lengthening, including the septum and tip.

    ① 30410
    ② 30430
    ③ 30460
    ④ 30462

23. Patient with suspected apnea underwent sleep study with recording of ventilation, respiratory effort, heart rate, and oxygen saturation. Technologist was in attendance.

    ① 95805
    ② 95806
    ③ 95807
    ④ 95811

24. Surgeon performed excision of pterygium with grafting, left eye.

    ① 65400
    ② 65420-LT
    ③ 65426-LT
    ④ 67800

25. The neonatologist was asked to be on standby for 35 minutes for cesarean delivery of baby in distress.

    ① 99360
    ② 99360 q = 2
    ③ 99464
    ④ 99465

26. Physician performed complex repair of a 3.2 cm scalp laceration.

    ① 13120
    ② 13120 + 13122
    ③ 13121
    ④ 13121 + 13122 q=1

27. A 65-year-old patient receives anesthesia for repair of inguinal hernia. The patient has controlled hypertension. Include physical status modifier with code.

    ① 00830-P1
    ② 00830-P2
    ③ 00832-P1
    ④ 00832-P2

28. The patient underwent creation of burr holes of the skull with evacuation of subdural hematoma.

    ① 61105
    ② 61140
    ③ 61154
    ④ 61156

29. A 5-year-old patient, status post eardrum rupture, undergoes tympanic membrane repair with patch.

    ① 69433
    ② 69610
    ③ 69620
    ④ 69631

30. David was scheduled to see Dr. Bronson for his six-month checkup and to have lab work done two weeks before his appointment on the 15th. As directed, the lab work was done on the first of the month. David called Dr. Bronson's office on the 3rd and talked to Dr. Bronson for 15 minutes about the tests. The doctor ordered two more tests done by the 5th so that the findings would be in the office for David's appointment on the 15th. What code would be reported for the service on the 3rd of the month?

    ① 99441
    ② 99442
    ③ 99443
    ④ 99444

31. Anesthesia was administered to the patient for gastric bypass procedure performed due to patient's morbid obesity. Include physical status modifier with code.

    ① 00700-P3
    ② 00790-P2
    ③ 00790-P3
    ④ 00797-P3

32. Physician performed excision of inguinal hidradenitis with complex repair.

    ① 11450
    ② 11451
    ③ 11462
    ④ 11463

33. Patient was scheduled to undergo extensive internal and external hemorrhoidectomy with fistulectomy. Ten minutes prior to the start of the procedure, after anesthesia had been administered, the patient experienced a rapid decrease in heart rate and the physician canceled the procedure.

    ① 46260
    ② 46260-52
    ③ 46260-53
    ④ 46262-53

34. Patient underwent cystourethroscopy and laser ablation of two bladder tumors, each approximately 2.7 cm in size.

    ① 52204
    ② 52214
    ③ 52234
    ④ 52235

35. Patient underwent excision of Peyronie plaque, with a 4.0 cm graft.

    ① 54060
    ② 54065
    ③ 54110
    ④ 54111

36. Hand specialist performs neuroplasty of the ulnar nerve of the left wrist

    ① 64704-LT
    ② 64718-LT
    ③ 64719-LT
    ④ 64721-LT

37. Patient, age 15, is seen by his new doctor for a comprehensive physical examination and immunizations. Patient also has moderate acne on face and chest.

    ① 99384
    ② 99384-25
    ③ 99394
    ④ 99394-25

38. Patient underwent replantation of thumb after complete amputation from the distal tip to the MP joint.

    ① 20816
    ② 20822
    ③ 20824
    ④ 20827

39. Patient underwent operative laryngoscopy for removal of chicken bone fragment.
    ① 31511
    ② 31525
    ③ 31530
    ④ 31531

40. Patient with history of hypertriglyceridemia but with normal cholesterol levels has triglyceride level determined.
    ① 82465
    ② 83718
    ③ 84478
    ④ 84485

41. Asthma patient receives initial evaluation and first IPPB treatment.
    ① 94640
    ② 94645
    ③ 94660
    ④ 94664

42. Dr. Ladwig performs an independent medical examination for patient Mr. Smith to determine Worker's Compensation impairment rating.
    ① 99450
    ② 99455
    ③ 99456
    ④ 99499

43. Patient receives anesthesia for extracorporeal shock wave lithotripsy with water bath. Patient has mild asthma. Include physical status modifier with code.
    ① 00872-P1
    ② 00872-P2
    ③ 00873-P1
    ④ 00873-P2

44. Patient underwent single-lung transplant with cardiopulmonary bypass employed during the procedure.
    ① 32851
    ② 32852
    ③ 32853
    ④ 32854

45. Patient with intestinal intussusception undergoes reduction through laparotomy approach.
    ① 44005
    ② 44020
    ③ 44050
    ④ 44055

46. Surgeon performs gastric bypass procedure for the patient's morbid obesity with small intestine reconstruction to limit absorption.
    ① 43842
    ② 43846
    ③ 43847
    ④ 43848

47. Ms. Jones was seen in an initial office orthopedic consultation for bilateral trochanteric bursitis; visit was considered problem-focused only.
    ① 99201
    ② 99241
    ③ 99242
    ④ 99251

48. Surgeon performs repair of abdominal aortic aneurysm, caused by high-grade atherosclerosis.
    ① 35001
    ② 35081
    ③ 35082
    ④ 35091

49. Dr. Kelly successfully performs resuscitation for an infant suffering from cardiac distress during delivery.
    ① 99461
    ② 99463
    ③ 99464
    ④ 99465

50. Patient underwent excision of 1.5 cm malignant skin lesion of the left calf, as well as removal of Norplant contraceptive capsules.
    ① 11602 + 11976
    ② 11602 + 11976-51
    ③ 11976 + 11602
    ④ 11976 + 11602-51

51. Patient was seen in the office for trigger point injection involving the trapezius and latissimus muscle groups.
    ① 20551
    ② 20552
    ③ 64415
    ④ 64420

52. Patient underwent hepatic artery ligation with complex suture repair of a liver laceration following motor vehicle accident.
    ① 47350
    ② 47360
    ③ 47360-51
    ④ 47361

53. Hospital follow-up visit by Dr. Stephens to see a 59-year-old female patient, status post uncomplicated left hip fixation.
    ① 99221
    ② 99223
    ③ 99231
    ④ 99232

54. Family practitioner performed excision of a lipoma of the right forearm, 1.5 cm in diameter.
    ① 11402
    ② 11402 + 12031
    ③ 11422
    ④ 11422 + 12031

55. Donor undergoes bone marrow harvesting for allogenic transplantation.
    ① 38220
    ② 38230
    ③ 38240
    ④ 38241

56. Patient underwent total gastrectomy with Roux-en-Y reconstruction for stomach carcinoma.
    ① 43620
    ② 43621
    ③ 43631
    ④ 43633

57. Surgeon performed a simple Burch urethropexy on a 45-year-old, mentally underdeveloped female.
    ① 51800
    ② 51840
    ③ 51841
    ④ 51992

58. Newly diagnosed testicular cancer patient underwent radical orchiectomy with abdominal exploration via inguinal approach.
    ① 54520
    ② 54522
    ③ 54530
    ④ 54535

59. Patient had reconstruction of the mandibular rami due to blunt trauma, undergoing C osteotomy with bone graft.

    ① 21188
    ② 21193
    ③ 21194
    ④ 21195

60. Patient underwent bilateral cerebral carotid angiography under direct radiologic supervision.

    ① 75665
    ② 75671
    ③ 75676
    ④ 75680

61. The patient was seen on initial comprehensive endocrinology office visit, having been referred for signs and symptoms of new-onset diabetes.

    ① 99201
    ② 99204
    ③ 99212
    ④ 99214

62. Patient underwent emergency laparoscopic appendectomy.

    ① 44950
    ② 44960
    ③ 44970
    ④ 44979

63. Patient underwent nephrolithotomy for removal of large staghorn calculus occupying the renal pelvis and calyces.

    ① 50010
    ② 50065
    ③ 50075
    ④ 50081

64. Patient underwent flexible sigmoidoscopy to 60 cm with removal of two small polyps using snare technique.

    ① 45330
    ② 45333
    ③ 45338
    ④ 45385

65. Dr. Roberts conducts a home visit for a non-ambulatory patient with progressive multiple sclerosis, now experiencing respiratory difficulty. The physician spent a total of 45 minutes with the new patient and family discussing treatment options and possible admission to nursing facility.

    ① 99342
    ② 99343
    ③ 99348
    ④ 99349

66. Surgeon performed limited thoracotomy for lung mass.

    ① 32096
    ② 32097
    ③ 32035
    ④ 32551

67. Patient underwent marsupialization of Bartholin gland cyst.

    ① 10040
    ② 10060
    ③ 56420
    ④ 56440

68. Patient receives 15 minutes of ultrasound therapy to the left hip for bursitis.

    ① 97033
    ② 97035
    ③ 97110
    ④ 97124

69. Patient with symptoms of poisoning underwent testing for the presence of arsenic.
    ① 82157
    ② 82175
    ③ 83015
    ④ 83018

70. Patient underwent pericardial window creation for drainage of excess pericardial fluid.
    ① 33010
    ② 33015
    ③ 33020
    ④ 33025

71. Patient with simple papilloma of the penis undergoes cryosurgical removal.
    ① 54056
    ② 54057
    ③ 54065
    ④ 54110

72. Pain specialist physician performs single lumbar epidural steroid injection.
    ① 62280
    ② 62282
    ③ 62311
    ④ 62319

73. Patient underwent emergency non-contrast head CT scan following blunt trauma to the skull.
    ① 70450
    ② 70470
    ③ 70486
    ④ 70540

74. Nuclear medicine ventilation and perfusion lung scan was performed on a patient with sudden shortness of breath; aerosol technique was used, two projections were obtained.
    ① 78579
    ② 78580
    ③ 78582
    ④ 78598

75. Patient was treated with femoral-popliteal venous bypass grafting for severe occlusive disease.
    ① 35450
    ② 35548
    ③ 35556
    ④ 35556 + 35500

76. A 12-year-old female patient underwent dilation of the urethra under general anesthesia.
    ① 53605
    ② 53660
    ③ 53661
    ④ 53665

77. Patient underwent radial keratotomy procedure in the right eye.
    ① 65710-RT
    ② 65760-RT
    ③ 65767-RT
    ④ 65771-RT

78. Combative patient underwent removal of burrowed insect from external auditory canal; general anesthesia required.
    ① 69145
    ② 69200
    ③ 69205
    ④ 69220

79. Expectant mother of twins underwent obstetrical ultrasound with fetal anatomic exam in her second trimester.
    ① 76805 + 76810
    ② 76811 + 76812
    ③ 76815
    ④ 76856

80. Patient Young, on parole, was to undergo his first monthly drug testing for marijuana. The lab ran a screen to detect the patient's THC level.
    ① 80100
    ② 80100 + 80101
    ③ 80101
    ④ 80104

81. Steelworker seen in the emergency room for acute eye pain associated with probable steel shaving in the affected eye, now gone.
    ① 99281
    ② 99283
    ③ 99284
    ④ 99285

82. Surgeon performs closure of rectovaginal fistula by vaginal approach.
    ① 57284
    ② 57300
    ③ 57305
    ④ 57310

83. Patient underwent before and after contrast MRI studies of the pelvis.
    ① 72191
    ② 72193
    ③ 72197
    ④ 72198

84. Surgeon performed open repair of a femoral neck fracture with internal fixation.
    ① 27230
    ② 27235
    ③ 27236
    ④ 27244

85. Patient underwent tubal occlusion with use of Falope rings, vaginal approach.
    ① 58600
    ② 58615
    ③ 58671
    ④ 58700

86. Patient receives chiropractic manipulative treatment for pain in the temporomandibular joint region.
    ① 97140
    ② 98925
    ③ 98940
    ④ 98943

87. Patient undergoes sex-change operation, from male to female.
    ① 55899
    ② 55970
    ③ 55980
    ④ 58999

88. Surgeon performed cesarean delivery after failed VBAC attempt.
    ① 59514
    ② 59610
    ③ 59612
    ④ 59620

89. Patient underwent cataract extraction with insertion of intraocular lens via phacoemulsification technique.
    ① 66830
    ② 66850
    ③ 66982
    ④ 66984

90. The CPT Category III codes are updated quarterly.
    ① True
    ② False

91. The doctor orders a urinalysis to screen for bacteria.
    ① 81000
    ② 81002
    ③ 81003
    ④ 81007

92. The patient has an automated CBC, WBC, and platelet count.
    ① 85025
    ② 85027
    ③ 85041
    ④ 85048

93. Dr. Roberts orders a test for total Hepatitis A antibodies.
    ① 86706
    ② 86707
    ③ 86708
    ④ 86709

94. The patient underwent debridement and dressing of a small burn of the forearm in Dr. Gray's office.
    ① 16000
    ② 16020
    ③ 16025
    ④ 16030

95. The patient underwent magnetic resonance imaging of the chest with before and after contrast studies to rule out a mass.
    ① 71550
    ② 71551
    ③ 71552
    ④ 71558

96. Mary Johnson had a closed manipulation of her distal fibular fracture.
    ① 27780
    ② 27786
    ③ 27788
    ④ 27792

97. The radiologist supervises and interprets lymphangiography of both upper arms.
    ① 75801-26
    ② 75803-26
    ③ 75805-26
    ④ 75807-26

98. Patient is hospitalized for a mobilization rearrangement repair of a conjunctival laceration.
    ① 65270
    ② 65272
    ③ 65273
    ④ 65285

99. The operative note states the patient underwent excision of a lesion of the mucosa and underlying muscle of the vestibule of the mouth.

    ① 40812
    ② 40814
    ③ 40816
    ④ 40820

100. Dr. Jones performed a C1-C2 anterior arthrodesis.

    ① 22548
    ② 22554 + 22585
    ③ 22595
    ④ 22600 + 22614

Name _____

Answers to Exam Questions: CPT

1. ① ② ③ ④	26. ① ② ③ ④	51. ① ② ③ ④	76. ① ② ③ ④
2. ① ② ③ ④	27. ① ② ③ ④	52. ① ② ③ ④	77. ① ② ③ ④
3. ① ② ③ ④	28. ① ② ③ ④	53. ① ② ③ ④	78. ① ② ③ ④
4. ① ② ③ ④	29. ① ② ③ ④	54. ① ② ③ ④	79. ① ② ③ ④
5. ① ② ③ ④	30. ① ② ③ ④	55. ① ② ③ ④	80. ① ② ③ ④
6. ① ② ③ ④	31. ① ② ③ ④	56. ① ② ③ ④	81. ① ② ③ ④
7. ① ② ③ ④	32. ① ② ③ ④	57. ① ② ③ ④	82. ① ② ③ ④
8. ① ② ③ ④	33. ① ② ③ ④	58. ① ② ③ ④	83. ① ② ③ ④
9. ① ② ③ ④	34. ① ② ③ ④	59. ① ② ③ ④	84. ① ② ③ ④
10. ① ② ③ ④	35. ① ② ③ ④	60. ① ② ③ ④	85. ① ② ③ ④
11. ① ② ③ ④	36. ① ② ③ ④	61. ① ② ③ ④	86. ① ② ③ ④
12. ① ② ③ ④	37. ① ② ③ ④	62. ① ② ③ ④	87. ① ② ③ ④
13. ① ② ③ ④	38. ① ② ③ ④	63. ① ② ③ ④	88. ① ② ③ ④
14. ① ② ③ ④	39. ① ② ③ ④	64. ① ② ③ ④	89. ① ② ③ ④
15. ① ② ③ ④	40. ① ② ③ ④	65. ① ② ③ ④	90. ① ②
16. ① ② ③ ④	41. ① ② ③ ④	66. ① ② ③ ④	91. ① ② ③ ④
17. ① ② ③ ④	42. ① ② ③ ④	67. ① ② ③ ④	92. ① ② ③ ④
18. ① ② ③ ④	43. ① ② ③ ④	68. ① ② ③ ④	93. ① ② ③ ④
19. ① ② ③ ④	44. ① ② ③ ④	69. ① ② ③ ④	94. ① ② ③ ④
20. ① ② ③ ④	45. ① ② ③ ④	70. ① ② ③ ④	95. ① ② ③ ④
21. ① ② ③ ④	46. ① ② ③ ④	71. ① ② ③ ④	96. ① ② ③ ④
22. ① ② ③ ④	47. ① ② ③ ④	72. ① ② ③ ④	97. ① ② ③ ④
23. ① ② ③ ④	48. ① ② ③ ④	73. ① ② ③ ④	98. ① ② ③ ④
24. ① ② ③ ④	49. ① ② ③ ④	74. ① ② ③ ④	99. ① ② ③ ④
25. ① ② ③ ④	50. ① ② ③ ④	75. ① ② ③ ④	100. ① ② ③ ④

Exam Questions for CPT and HCPCS

Name _____

Directions: Use the appropriate coding manual to determine the correct choice for each situation.

1. To report ambulance services for a Medicare patient ordered by a physician, use modifier:
   ① –QM
   ② –QN
   ③ –RC
   ④ –RT

2. A patient underwent simple incision and drainage of an abscess on his thigh. The wound was packed with iodoform gauze (approximately 2 × 2). Select the correct codes for the procedure and the gauze.
   ① 10060 + A6220
   ② 10060 + A6222
   ③ 10061 + A6222
   ④ 10061 + A6223

3. HCPCS Level II codes are four-position alphanumeric codes used to represent items not represented in Level I (CPT) codes.
   ① True
   ② False

4. A patient is to undergo an IVP but has a severe reaction to the contrast material and the IVP procedure is discontinued. Which modifier is used to describe this situation?
   ① –22
   ② –52
   ③ –53
   ④ –56

5. A patient was seen in the urgent care center with signs and symptoms of dehydration. She was observed for 8 hours while receiving IV normal saline infusion, 1000 cc. Select the correct HCPCS code for the infusion.
   ① J7030
   ② J7040
   ③ J7050
   ④ J7120

6. The L group of codes represents which procedures/products?
   ① Pathology and laboratory
   ② Drugs and enterals
   ③ Orthotics and prosthetics
   ④ Speech and language services

7. In CPT coding, the history, examination, and medical decision making are considered the key components in selecting the level of E/M services.
   ① True
   ② False

8. If a patient has trigger thumb release performed on the right, which modifier is used for the anatomic location?
   ① –F4
   ② –F5
   ③ –F9
   ④ –FA

135

9. A nursing facility patient developed multiple decubitus ulcers after a hospital stay. Her physician readmitted her to the nursing facility, did a detailed exam, developed a new plan of care, and ordered an air-fluidized bed for treatment. Select the correct E/M and HCPCS codes.

   ① 99304 + E0193
   ② 99304 + E0194
   ③ 99305 + E0193
   ④ 99305 + E0194

10. The use of HCPCS codes is mandatory on all Medicare and Medicaid claims submitted for payment for services of allied health care professionals.

    ① True
    ② False

11. A patient was seen in consultation for possible surgery. The surgeon schedules the procedure for the following day. Which modifier would you choose to indicate the decision for surgery?

    ① –54
    ② –55
    ③ –56
    ④ –57

12. Select the correct HCPCS code for an insertion tray without drainage bag or catheter.

    ① A4310
    ② A4311
    ③ A4312
    ④ A4313

13. Select the correct HCPCS code for surgical stockings, below-knee length.

    ① A4490
    ② A4495
    ③ A4500
    ④ A4510

14. In CPT coding, the definition of outpatient services would be those provided to a person who has not been admitted as an inpatient to a facility.

    ① True
    ② False

15. A patient has incision and drainage of an abscess involving the left fourth toe. Identify the correct modifier.

    ① –T2
    ② –T3
    ③ –T6
    ④ –T8

16. The patient was seen in the office for a facial chemical peel, epidermal only.

    ① 15780
    ② 15786
    ③ 15788
    ④ 15789

17. K codes in HCPCS represent the official codes for durable medical equipment.

    ① True
    ② False

18. The patient was seen in the emergency department for acute shortness of breath. During his observation in the emergency department, multiple arterial blood gas testing was performed to monitor his improvement. Which modifier would you choose to accurately code the multiple ABGs?

    ① –51
    ② –90
    ③ –91
    ④ –99

19. Select the correct HCPCS code for a tourniquet used by a dialysis patient.
   ① A4911
   ② A4913
   ③ A4918
   ④ A4929

20. Select the correct HCPCS code for a pair of aluminum underarm crutches.
   ① E0110
   ② E0112
   ③ E0114
   ④ E0116

21. Physical status modifiers in CPT are used to distinguish the varying levels of complexity of surgical services provided.
   ① True
   ② False

22. A Medicare patient received a wheelchair two months ago, but the beneficiary has not decided whether to purchase or rent. Which HCPCS modifier would you use?
   ① –BO
   ② –BP
   ③ –BR
   ④ –BU

23. A teenage patient, new to the practice, was seen in a problem-focused visit for symptoms of tonsillitis and pharyngitis. She was given an injection of azithromycin for her acute symptoms. Select the correct E/M code and the HCPCS code.
   ① 99201 + J0290
   ② 99201 + J0456
   ③ 99202 + J0290
   ④ 99202 + J0456

24. It is acceptable to code HCPCS from index entries only.
   ① True
   ② False

25. A patient was seen by her family doctor for a routine physical exam. During the exam, the patient was noted to have high blood pressure. The physician discussed the new finding with the patient, and the patient disclosed she has been under a great deal of stress due to the demands of her work and impending divorce. The high blood pressure was deemed stress-related and the physician and the patient discussed stress-reduction techniques. As a result of the extended discussion with the patient, the visit was prolonged beyond the normally expected length for a routine physical exam. Which CPT modifier would you use to document the additional time spent with the patient?
   ① –P3
   ② –22
   ③ –24
   ④ –25

26. Select the correct HCPCS code for a surgically implanted electrical osteogenesis stimulator.
   ① E0748
   ② E0749
   ③ E0760
   ④ E0761

27. Select the correct HCPCS code to report a patient receiving an injection of amphotericin B, 50 mg.
   ① J0285
   ② J0287 q = 5
   ③ J0288 q = 5
   ④ J0289 q = 5

28. The general definition of the CPT surgical package includes the patient's preoperative evaluation on the day of the procedure, the surgical procedure and its usual components, and the patient's uncomplicated follow-up care.

    ① True
    ② False

29. The patient had a skin tag removed from her upper right eyelid. Which HCPCS modifier describes this location?

    ① –E1
    ② –E2
    ③ –E3
    ④ –E4

30. An infant born with clubfoot on the right was seen in the pediatric orthopedic clinic as a new patient. The physician conducted a problem-focused history and examination and prescribed a clubfoot wedge for the patient. Select the correct codes for the visit and the wedge.

    ① 99201 + L3201-RT
    ② 99201 + L3380-RT
    ③ 99212 + L3201-RT
    ④ 99212 + L3380-RT

31. The HCPCS route of administration "JA" means the patient is receiving the drug intravenously.

    ① True
    ② False

32. The patient was seen in the office for exercise stress testing. When the physician was placing the EKG leads, she noticed a suspicious mole on the patient's chest and excised the lesion. What CPT modifier would you use to indicate the additional procedure performed during this visit?

    ① –50
    ② –51
    ③ –52
    ④ –53

33. A patient was seen in the office for acute hives. The doctor gave her a 25-mg injection of hydroxyzine. Select the correct HCPCS code.

    ① J3400
    ② J3410
    ③ J3470
    ④ J3485

34. Select the correct HCPCS code for an orthopedic shoe insole made of felt and covered with leather.

    ① L3500
    ② L3520
    ③ L3540
    ④ L3570

35. To measure and code the removal of a lesion using CPT guidelines, the lesion size must be expressed in inches.

    ① True
    ② False

36. If a patient is prescribed oxygen therapy at 0.5 liters per minute, which HCPCS modifier describes this flow rate?

    ① –QE
    ② –QF
    ③ –QG
    ④ –QH

37. An established patient was seen in the office because of difficulty toileting after hip replacement surgery. The physician examined the patient and sent her home with a stationary commode chair with fixed arms to use during her recovery period. Select the appropriate codes.

    ① 99211 + E0163
    ② 99211 + E0165
    ③ 99212 + E0163
    ④ 99212 + E0165

38. All HCPCS codes and descriptions are updated monthly by CMS.

    ① True

    ② False

39. Which CPT modifier would you choose to indicate a patient received a service or procedure that was less than originally intended?

    ① –22

    ② –32

    ③ –51

    ④ –52

40. Select the correct HCPCS code that describes the reduction of an ocular prosthesis.

    ① V2623

    ② V2625

    ③ V2626

    ④ V2629

41. A patient was given an intramuscular injection of 2 mg of Haldol in the physician's office. Select the correct HCPCS code.

    ① J1630

    ② J1631

    ③ J3410

    ④ J3470

42. When coding bilateral procedures in CPT, you must always include the code 09950.

    ① True

    ② False

43. The mobile x-ray service came to the nursing facility to x-ray Mrs. Jones for possible hip fracture. The x-ray will be interpreted tomorrow by the radiologist. Which HCPCS modifier would you use for today's service?

    ① –TA

    ② –TC

    ③ –TD

    ④ –TE

44. A Medicare patient with diabetes saw the doctor for routine foot care: the trimming of three calluses and debridement of all 10 toenails.

    ① 11056 + 11719

    ② 11056 + 11721

    ③ 11057 + 11720

    ④ S0390

45. Laboratory services in HCPCS are listed in the P codes grouping.

    ① True

    ② False

46. Which CPT modifier would you use to indicate that an outside laboratory was used to process a patient's specimen?

    ① –56

    ② –90

    ③ –91

    ④ –99

47. Select the correct HCPCS code for a patient receiving non-emergency minibus transportation in a mountain area.

    ① A0080

    ② A0110

    ③ A0120

    ④ A0160

48. Many radiology procedures include two parts: a technical component and a professional component.

    ① True

    ② False

49. A patient has used his wheelchair for nearly 4 years. Due to wear, he now needs a replacement for the right footrest. Which HCPCS modifier is used to indicate this replacement?

   ① –RB
   ② –RC
   ③ –RR
   ④ –RT

50. A patient was referred to the office of a wound care specialist for consultation regarding his non-healing surgical wound. The physician spent approximately 30 minutes with the patient and sent him home on topical hyperbaric oxygen chamber therapy for wound healing. Select the correct codes.

   ① 99241 + A4575
   ② 99242 + A4575
   ③ 99251 + A4575
   ④ 99252 + A4575

51. Drugs listed in HCPCS are identified by both brand and generic names.

   ① True
   ② False

52. A patient underwent emergency cholecystectomy 6 days after having a lung biopsy. The same surgeon performed both procedures. Which CPT modifier is used on the second surgery to indicate this type of situation?

   ① –58
   ② –59
   ③ –78
   ④ –79

53. Which of the following HCPCS code groups are listed for use only on a temporary basis?

   ① G, J, Q
   ② G, K, Q
   ③ J, K, S
   ④ K, P, S

54. A patient was seen for insertion of a temporary indwelling latex Foley urinary catheter. Select the correct codes.

   ① 51701 + A4314
   ② 51701 + A4338
   ③ 51702 + A4338
   ④ 51703 + A4328

55. According to CPT coding guidelines, a pathology consultation includes a medical interpretive report.

   ① True
   ② False

56. Dr. Wilkins amputated a patient's right lower extremity (BKA). His staff PA was the assistant during the procedure. Which HCPCS modifier would you choose to indicate the PA's role in this procedure?

   ① –AD
   ② –AM
   ③ –AS
   ④ –AT

57. A patient was seen by the nurse for a routine visit in the multiple sclerosis clinic. The patient received an injection of beta-1a interferon, 30 mcg, from the nurse in the clinic. Select the appropriate codes.

   ① 99211 + J1826
   ② 99211 + J9212
   ③ 99212 + J1826
   ④ 99212 + J9214

58. HCPCS ambulance modifiers always include one alpha character and one numeric character.

   ① True
   ② False

59. A patient suddenly refuses to have surgery performed after being prepped for the procedure and just before receiving the anesthesia. Which CPT modifier would you use to indicate the change in plans?

    ① –52
    ② –53
    ③ –56
    ④ None of the above

60. Select the correct HCPCS code for a drainable rubber ostomy pouch with a faceplate attached.

    ① A4375
    ② A4376
    ③ A4377
    ④ A4378

61. Select the correct HCPCS code for replacement handgrip for a cane that the patient owns.

    ① A4635
    ② A4636
    ③ A4637
    ④ A4640

62. In CPT coding, when the patient receives an immune globulin product, you must also include an administration code as appropriate.

    ① True
    ② False

63. An ambulance was called to come to the aid of a choking patient; however, the patient expired before the ambulance arrived on the scene. Which HCPCS modifier would you use to document this circumstance?

    ① –QK
    ② –QL
    ③ –QM
    ④ –QP

64. Patient underwent unattended sleep study with monitoring of oxygen saturation and chest movement. The patient was not able to sleep adequately throughout the study and therefore the study was equivocal. The patient was provided with a recording apnea monitor for home use. Select the appropriate codes.

    ① 95806 + E0618
    ② 95806 + E0619
    ③ 95807 + E0618
    ④ 95807 + E0619

65. The two levels of national HCPCS codes can be applied to both inpatient and outpatient services by physicians.

    ① True
    ② False

66. Which CPT modifier is used to indicate a repeat procedure performed by a different physician?

    ① –58
    ② –76
    ③ –77
    ④ –78

67. Select the correct HCPCS code for a hydrogel dressing with an adhesive border used to cover a 24-square inch wound.

    ① A6242
    ② A6243
    ③ A6246
    ④ A6247

68. Select the correct HCPCS code for home mix parenteral nutritional additives, to include electrolytes.

    ① B4197
    ② B4199
    ③ B4216
    ④ B4220

69. When coding in CPT, no distinction is made between new and established patients in the emergency department.

    ① True
    ② False

70. A patient was seen in the contraceptive clinic two weeks after delivery of her child. She was fitted with a copper intrauterine device. Select the codes for the fitting and the device.

    ① 58300 + J7303
    ② 58300 + J7300
    ③ 58301 + J7303
    ④ 58301 + J7300

71. Select the correct HCPCS code for a replacement brake attachment on a wheeled walker.

    ① E0143
    ② E0147
    ③ E0155
    ④ E0159

72. Select the correct HCPCS code for a patient admitted as an inpatient to a residential addiction program for acute alcohol detoxification.

    ① H0009
    ② H0011
    ③ H0012
    ④ H0013

73. A patient was fitted with a 2-lead TENS unit for pain control after suffering a fractured radius. Select appropriate codes.

    ① 64550 + E0720
    ② 64550 + E0730
    ③ 64575 + E0720
    ④ 64575 + E0730

74. Select the correct HCPCS code for an injection of methylprednisolone acetate, 40 mg.

    ① J1020 q = 2
    ② J1030
    ③ J1040
    ④ J1051

75. A patient came to the office to have a B12 level analysis and to receive her weekly B12 shot. Select the correct codes.

    ① 82607 + J3420
    ② 82607 + J3430
    ③ 82608 + J3420
    ④ 82608 + J3430

76. Select the HCPCS code that correctly identifies a unit of leukocyte-reduced platelets.

    ① P9019
    ② P9020
    ③ P9031
    ④ P9034

77. Select the correct HCPCS code for 1 mg of inhaled dexamethasone in concentrated form.

    ① J1094
    ② J1100
    ③ J7637
    ④ J7638

78. A patient who is status post left-sided CVA was seen for weight loss and other symptoms indicative of dysphagia. She received dysphagia screening and her first treatment for the swallowing dysfunction. Select the correct codes.

    ① 92526 + V5362
    ② 92526 + V5364
    ③ 92610 + V5362
    ④ 92610 + V5364

79. Select the correct HCPCS code for a non-heated humidifier used with a positive airway pressure device.

   ① A7039
   ② E0550
   ③ E0560
   ④ E0561

80. The physician spent 30 minutes with the patient and family to discuss discharge plans on the day of discharge, as well as the patient's immediate at-home care. The patient had undergone his second below-knee amputation, and was given a transfer board for use at home. Select the codes for the discharge visit and the transfer board.

   ① 99238 + E0705
   ② 99238 + E1035
   ③ 99239 + E0705
   ④ 99239 + E1035

81. Select the correct HCPCS code that reflects the supply of a one-dose vial of technetium Tc 99m disofenin.

   ① A9500
   ② A9502
   ③ A9510
   ④ A9536

82. Identify the HCPCS code that describes a full-leg, segmental pneumatic appliance with compressor.

   ① E0650
   ② E0660
   ③ E0667
   ④ E0671

83. Select the HCPCS code for a 50-mg intravenous infusion of cisplatin in the physician's office.

   ① J0743
   ② J0770
   ③ J9060 q = 5
   ④ J9070

84. To report the services of one CRNA directed by the anesthesiologist for the fifth procedure supervised by that physician, use modifier:

   ① –QS
   ② –QX
   ③ –QY
   ④ –QZ

85. To report the services of the anesthesiologist in question 84, use modifier:

   ① –AA
   ② –AD
   ③ –QK
   ④ –QY

86. At the physician's direction, the RN called the patient at home to monitor the patient's program for control of her severe arthritis.

   ① S0220
   ② S0271
   ③ S0315
   ④ S0320

87. A patient was fitted with a custom-made compression burn garment for severe burns of the chest and upper back.

   ① A6501
   ② A6509
   ③ A6510
   ④ A6511

88. A patient with a fractured femur and tibia had a trapeze and grab bar attached to a hospital bed in his home.

   ① E0910
   ② E0920
   ③ E0940
   ④ E0941

89. Five patients participated in the group psychotherapy session and received educational materials.

   ① 90806 + 99071
   ② 90846 + 99070
   ③ 90853 + 99071
   ④ 90901 + 99070

90. A 68-year-old male received a drainable ostomy pouch with an attached barrier.

   ① A5051
   ② A5054
   ③ A5061
   ④ A5071

91. The patient got a replacement for a lost gas permeable bifocal contact lens.

   ① V2430
   ② V2502
   ③ V2512
   ④ V2522

92. The codes in HCPCS that are not reported to Medicare are the ones that begin with the letters:

   ① B, E, H, S
   ② G, H, T
   ③ H, S, T
   ④ H, K, S, T

93. A defined formula (100 calories to a unit) to meet a special metabolic need when administered through a feeding tube is reported with code:

   ① B4150
   ② B4152
   ③ B4153
   ④ B4154

94. Dr. Johnson serves a large rural area and some patients request their E/M services via the Internet. These documented encounters would be reported with code:

   ① 99056
   ② 99347
   ③ 99441
   ④ 99444

95. The infant with a left club foot was treated by manipulation and a short leg cast.

   ① 29405-LT
   ② 29425-LT
   ③ 29450-LT
   ④ 29799-LT

96. Mary's mother and sister have known BRCA1 mutation and she now undergoes testing for the mutation.

   ① S3818
   ② S3820
   ③ S3822
   ④ S3823

97. A shoe store specializing in diabetic shoes supplied a patient with a pair that had a metatarsal bar.

   ① A5500 q = 2
   ② A5503 q = 2
   ③ A5504 q = 2
   ④ A5505 q = 2

98. Following his hospitalization, the patient went home with cervical traction equipment that fit over a door.

   ① E0840
   ② E0850
   ③ E0860
   ④ E0870

99. The patient was authorized to receive a new 12 volt battery charger.

① L7360

② L7362

③ L7364

④ L7366

100. A patient received 1 g of Gammagard liquid immune globulin intravenously from the nurse in his doctor's office, 45 minutes.

① 90281 + J1460

② 90281 + J1559

③ 90471 + J1559

④ 96365 + J1569 q = 2

Name _____

Answers to Exam Questions: CPT and HCPCS

1. ① ② ③ ④
2. ① ② ③ ④
3. ① ②
4. ① ② ③ ④
5. ① ② ③ ④
6. ① ② ③ ④
7. ① ②
8. ① ② ③ ④
9. ① ② ③ ④
10. ① ②
11. ① ② ③ ④
12. ① ② ③ ④
13. ① ② ③ ④
14. ① ②
15. ① ② ③ ④
16. ① ② ③ ④
17. ① ②
18. ① ② ③ ④
19. ① ② ③ ④
20. ① ② ③ ④
21. ① ②
22. ① ② ③ ④
23. ① ② ③ ④
24. ① ②
25. ① ② ③ ④

26. ① ② ③ ④
27. ① ② ③ ④
28. ① ②
29. ① ② ③ ④
30. ① ② ③ ④
31. ① ②
32. ① ② ③ ④
33. ① ② ③ ④
34. ① ② ③ ④
35. ① ②
36. ① ② ③ ④
37. ① ② ③ ④
38. ① ②
39. ① ② ③ ④
40. ① ② ③ ④
41. ① ② ③ ④
42. ① ②
43. ① ② ③ ④
44. ① ② ③ ④
45. ① ②
46. ① ② ③ ④
47. ① ② ③ ④
48. ① ②
49. ① ② ③ ④
50. ① ② ③ ④

51. ① ②
52. ① ② ③ ④
53. ① ② ③ ④
54. ① ② ③ ④
55. ① ②
56. ① ② ③ ④
57. ① ② ③ ④
58. ① ②
59. ① ② ③ ④
60. ① ② ③ ④
61. ① ② ③ ④
62. ① ②
63. ① ② ③ ④
64. ① ② ③ ④
65. ① ②
66. ① ② ③ ④
67. ① ② ③ ④
68. ① ② ③ ④
69. ① ②
70. ① ② ③ ④
71. ① ② ③ ④
72. ① ② ③ ④
73. ① ② ③ ④
74. ① ② ③ ④
75. ① ② ③ ④

76. ① ② ③ ④
77. ① ② ③ ④
78. ① ② ③ ④
79. ① ② ③ ④
80. ① ② ③ ④
81. ① ② ③ ④
82. ① ② ③ ④
83. ① ② ③ ④
84. ① ② ③ ④
85. ① ② ③ ④
86. ① ② ③ ④
87. ① ② ③ ④
88. ① ② ③ ④
89. ① ② ③ ④
90. ① ② ③ ④
91. ① ② ③ ④
92. ① ② ③ ④
93. ① ② ③ ④
94. ① ② ③ ④
95. ① ② ③ ④
96. ① ② ③ ④
97. ① ② ③ ④
98. ① ② ③ ④
99. ① ② ③ ④
100. ① ② ③ ④

Exam Questions for ICD-9-CM

Directions: Use the appropriate coding manual to determine the correct choice for each situation.

1. A patient seen in the office today has known Graves' disease, now with signs and symptoms of a thyroid storm.
   ① 242.01
   ② 242.20
   ③ 242.90
   ④ 242.91

2. A three-year-old patient was brought in by her mother because of fever, fussiness, and tugging at the right ear. Otoscopy confirmed acute infection, with erythema and pus of the canal.
   ① 380.10
   ② 381.00
   ③ 381.10
   ④ 382.00

3. A patient was seen because of pain and swelling of the right elbow. The joint does not appear to be unstable. Rule out fracture.
   ① 719.02
   ② 719.42 + 719.02
   ③ 812.20
   ④ 812.40

4. A patient took the ampicillin as directed but returns to the office today with urticaria and swelling, classic signs of allergic reaction.
   ① 708.0
   ② 708.0 + 995.27 + E930.0
   ③ 708.0 + 995.20 + E930.0
   ④ 708.0 + E930.0

5. Newly diagnosed asthma patient was counseled regarding asthma therapy and the correct use of a nebulizer.
   ① V65.2
   ② V65.40
   ③ V65.49
   ④ V65.8

6. Select the correct code for ulcerative impetigo caused by a superficial staph infection.
   ① 111.9
   ② 684
   ③ 686.00
   ④ 694.3

7. Patient was seen for evaluation of pilonidal cyst.
   ① 173.50
   ② 685.0
   ③ 685.1
   ④ 686.00

8. Patient came to the office for examination of a penile lesion; physician determined it is a classic plaque of Peyronie's disease.
   ① 607.85
   ② 607.89
   ③ 608.89
   ④ 608.9

9. Patient was seen for annual gynecological exam including Pap smear.
   ① V70.0 + V76.2
   ② V70.9
   ③ V72.31 + V76.2
   ④ V76.2

149

10. Visit regarding contraceptive use; patient received Norplant contraceptive one month ago.
    ① V25.09
    ② V25.40
    ③ V25.43
    ④ V65.40

11. Patient fell while snowboarding, suffering a dislocation of the left shoulder.
    ① 831.00
    ② 831.00 + E885.4
    ③ 831.09
    ④ 831.19 + E885.4

12. Select the correct code for a bilateral, non-strangulated inguinal hernia.
    ① 550.10
    ② 550.90
    ③ 550.92
    ④ 550.93

13. Patient was seen for vaginal spotting in her 21st week of pregnancy.
    ① 623.8
    ② 640.03
    ③ 640.93
    ④ 649.53

14. A 35-year-old female was seen in the office today for evaluation of a breast lump.
    ① 610.1
    ② 611.0
    ③ 611.2
    ④ 611.72

15. A 16-year-old male was seen in the clinic for severe sore throat, redness, cough, and erythema. Rapid strep test was positive.
    ① 034
    ② 034.0
    ③ 462 + 034.0
    ④ 463

16. Select the correct code for personal history of cervical carcinoma.
    ① 180.9
    ② 233.1
    ③ V10.40
    ④ V10.41

17. Patient was seen for continuing treatment of post-traumatic stress disorder.
    ① 309.0
    ② 309.81
    ③ 309.83
    ④ 309.9

18. Patient was diagnosed with bulimia.
    ① 307.50
    ② 307.51
    ③ 783.0
    ④ 783.6

19. Patient complains of diarrhea, abdominal cramping, and bloody stools. Rule out ulcerative colitis.
    ① 556.9
    ② 556.9 + 578.1 + 787.91
    ③ 578.1 + 787.91 + 789.00
    ④ 787.91

20. Child was seen for erythema and puncture wounds of the right forearm due to cat bite.

    ① 880.03

    ② 881.00

    ③ 881.00 + E906.3

    ④ E906.3

21. Patient came to the office to discuss treatment options for new diagnosis of malignant melanoma of the forehead.

    ① 172.0

    ② 172.3

    ③ 172.8

    ④ 172.9

22. Infant was brought in for evaluation of skin tags of the outer ear/earlobe.

    ① 744.1

    ② 744.29

    ③ 757.39

    ④ 757.8

23. Patient's daughter brought her father in for follow-up of progressive Alzheimer's dementia.

    ① 294.10

    ② 294.8

    ③ 331.0

    ④ 331.0 + 294.10

24. Child was brought into the office for evaluation and examination after swallowing a dime.

    ① 933.0

    ② 934.8

    ③ 935.2

    ④ 938

25. Vacationing patient was seen in the urgent care clinic for second-degree sunburn of both shoulder areas.

    ① 692.74

    ② 692.76

    ③ 692.82

    ④ 692.89

26. Select the correct code for Lyme disease.

    ① 088.0

    ② 088.81

    ③ 088.89

    ④ 088.9

27. Patient came into the office seeking treatment for fungal toenail infection.

    ① 110.1

    ② 110.8

    ③ 681.11

    ④ 681.9

28. Patient was seen in the office today requesting medications to assist with alcohol withdrawal.

    ① 291.0

    ② 291.4

    ③ 291.81

    ④ 291.89

29. Patient was seen for follow-up of long finger amputated in home workshop, now replanted.

    ① 883.0

    ② 884.0

    ③ 886.0

    ④ 886.1

30. A six-year-old patient was brought in for additional testing for color blindness.

    ① 368.55

    ② 368.59

    ③ 368.60

    ④ 368.8

31. Patient was evaluated for somnolence relating to reactive hypoglycemia.
    ① 251.1
    ② 251.1 + 780.09
    ③ 251.2 + 780.02
    ④ 251.2 + 780.09

32. Select the correct code(s) for malignant hypertensive heart disease with chronic renal failure.
    ① 401.0 + 593.9
    ② 403.90 + 586
    ③ 403.00 + 585.9
    ④ 405.01

33. Patient was seen for preoperative cardiovascular evaluation prior to undergoing cholecystectomy.
    ① V72.81
    ② V72.83
    ③ V72.85
    ④ V72.9

34. Patient was seen in follow-up for Bennett's fracture of the right extremity.
    ① 814.00
    ② 815.00
    ③ 815.01
    ④ 815.10

35. Select the correct code(s) for cellulitis of the colostomy site.
    ① 569.60
    ② 569.61 + 682.2
    ③ 682.2 + 041.10
    ④ 998.59

36. Select the correct code for congenital bowleggedness.
    ① 736.42
    ② 736.5
    ③ 754.40
    ④ 754.44

37. Patient was seen by the gastroenterologist for evaluation of prolapsed internal hemorrhoids and anal fissure.
    ① 455.1 + 565.0
    ② 455.2 + 565.0
    ③ 455.5 + 565.1
    ④ 455.8 + 565.0

38. Patient was seen in the office for severe vertigo and loss of hearing. The patient was diagnosed with viral labyrinthitis.
    ① 386.19
    ② 386.30
    ③ 386.35
    ④ 780.4

39. Select the correct code(s) for idiopathic scoliosis with backache.
    ① 724.5
    ② 737.30
    ③ 737.30 + 724.5
    ④ 737.43

40. Patient was evaluated for varicose veins with stasis dermatitis of the left lower extremity.
    ① 447.2
    ② 451.0
    ③ 453.52
    ④ 454.1

41. A 20-year-old patient was seen for continuing evaluation of Turner's syndrome.
    ① 752.7
    ② 758.6
    ③ 758.7
    ④ 758.89

42. Patient was seen with complaints of melena and anemia. Patient has strong family history of stomach cancer.

    ① 578.1 + 280.9 + V10.04
    ② 578.1 + 280.9 + V16.0
    ③ 578.9 + 280.9 + V16.0
    ④ V16.0

43. Select the correct codes for diabetic cataracts.

    ① 250.50 + 366.41
    ② 250.50 + 366.9
    ③ 250.51 + 366.41
    ④ 250.51 + 366.09

44. Patient was seen in follow-up for right bundle-branch block with incomplete left bundle-branch block.

    ① 426.4 + 426.3
    ② 426.51
    ③ 426.53
    ④ 426.54

45. The patient is status post PTCA, in for a one-week follow-up visit.

    ① V45.81
    ② V45.82
    ③ V67.00
    ④ V67.9

46. Patient was seen for complaints of fatigue and was noted to have diffuse adenopathy. Ruleout leukemia.

    ① 208.00
    ② 208.80
    ③ 785.6 + 208.00
    ④ 785.6 + 780.79

47. Patient's chief complaint is losing her sense of smell after a bout of the flu.

    ① 349.9
    ② 781.1
    ③ 782.0
    ④ 799.29

48. Patient was seen for treatment of situational depression due to impending divorce.

    ① 308.3
    ② 309.0
    ③ 309.1
    ④ 309.24

49. Select the correct code for acquired trigger finger.

    ① 727.03
    ② 727.09
    ③ 756.89
    ④ 756.9

50. Select the correct code for rupture of theAchilles tendon.

    ① 726.71
    ② 727.50
    ③ 727.60
    ④ 727.67

51. Patient was seen for vaginal bleeding; placenta previa was detected. Patient is in early second trimester of pregnancy.

    ① 640.03
    ② 641.03
    ③ 641.10
    ④ 641.13

52. Select the correct code for narcolepsy.

    ① 301.81
    ② 307.45
    ③ 347.00
    ④ 780.50

53. Patient had episodes of "zoning out" and, after extensive observation and testing, was diagnosed with absence seizures.

    ① 345.00
    ② 345.01
    ③ 345.10
    ④ 345.40

54. Child was found to have a severe allergy to dog hair.

    ① 477.0
    ② 477.2
    ③ 477.9
    ④ 478.11

55. Patient was seen for treatment of frostbite of the toes.

    ① 991.2
    ② 991.3
    ③ 991.5
    ④ 991.6

56. Patient received an accidental, self-inflicted laceration of the palm of his hand while using a kitchen knife.

    ① 880.03 + E920.3
    ② 882.0 + E920.3
    ③ 882.0 + E920.8
    ④ 883.0 + E920.3

57. Patient was seen in consultation for several episodes of hydrocodone addiction.

    ① 304.02
    ② 304.62
    ③ 304.72
    ④ 305.42

58. Patient visiting from out of state was treated for headache, nausea, and vomiting. The patient was diagnosed with altitude sickness.

    ① 784.0
    ② 787.01
    ③ 993.2
    ④ E902.0

59. Select the correct code for acute viral conjunctivitis.

    ① 032.81
    ② 077.4
    ③ 077.99
    ④ 372.03

60. Select the correct codes for accidental poisoning with whiskey.

    ① 980.0 + E860.0
    ② 980.0 + E860.1
    ③ 980.9 + E860.2
    ④ 980.9 + E860.0

61. Patient returns to the office for ongoing evaluation of dysphasia. He suffered a cerebrovascular accident 6 months ago.

    ① 438.12
    ② 438.19
    ③ 784.49
    ④ 784.59

62. Select the correct codes for metastatic carcinoma of the liver with unknown primary.

    ① 155.0 + 239.0
    ② 197.7 + 199.1
    ③ 197.7 + 155.0
    ④ 197.7 + 239.0

63. The patient was seen in the office for complaints of halitosis.
    ① 783.9
    ② 784.49
    ③ 784.99
    ④ 786.30

64. Select the correct code for central corneal ulcer probably due to improper contact lens use and care.
    ① 370.00
    ② 370.03
    ③ 370.33
    ④ 370.49

65. The patient was seen by the orthopedic physician regarding carpal tunnel syndrome.
    ① 354.0
    ② 354.2
    ③ 354.8
    ④ 354.9

66. The patient suffered a severe burn over one year ago and is being evaluated for continued neuropathy of the left thigh secondary to the burn.
    ① 353.6 + 906.8
    ② 355.71 + 906.7
    ③ 355.8 + 906.7
    ④ 355.8 + 906.8

67. Patient was seen in the office for pain due to phantom limb syndrome.
    ① 353.4
    ② 353.6
    ③ 353.8
    ④ 353.9

68. Select the correct code for arteriovenous malformation of the right lower extremity requiring surgical treatment.
    ① 747.49
    ② 747.60
    ③ 747.64
    ④ 757.9

69. Infant was seen in the office today for follow-up of Tetrology of Fallot.
    ① 745.10
    ② 745.2
    ③ 746.09
    ④ 746.4

70. Patient is being treated in the hospital for severe mitral regurgitation.
    ① 394.9
    ② 396.0
    ③ 424.0
    ④ 424.1

71. Patient was treated for a laceration and puncture wound of the right nostril; fish hook accidentally embedded in nostril.
    ① 873.20 + E920.8
    ② 873.22 + E920.8
    ③ 873.29 + E920.9
    ④ 873.39 + E920.8

72. Select the correct code for South American pemphigus.
    ① 694.4
    ② 694.60
    ③ 757.39
    ④ 785.4

73. Patient returns to the office for physical therapy to regain strength in his back after a thoracic muscle strain at work.
    ① 847.1 + V57.1
    ② 847.9 + V57.1
    ③ V57.1 + 847.1
    ④ V57.89 + 847.1

74. Select the correct code for temporomandibular joint syndrome (TMJ).
    ① 524.4
    ② 524.60
    ③ 524.69
    ④ 524.9

75. Patient was seen for evaluation and treatment of neurogenic bladder.
    ① 596.4
    ② 596.53
    ③ 596.54
    ④ 596.89

76. Patient came to the office with urinary symptoms. On digital exam, the patient was found to have a multinodular prostate gland.
    ① 600.00
    ② 600.10
    ③ 600.3
    ④ 600.91

77. The patient was seen today for weekly chemotherapy infusion; recent diagnosis of primary carcinoma of the descending colon.
    ① V58.11 + 153.2
    ② V58.11 + 235.2
    ③ V66.2 + 153.2
    ④ V66.2 + 235.2

78. Patient is being seen for acute reactive depression due to recent diagnosis of pancreatic cancer.
    ① 289.9 + 239.0
    ② 300.4 + 157.1
    ③ 300.4 + 157.9
    ④ 300.4 + 239.0

79. Select the correct code for acute sinusitis in conjunction with influenza.
    ① 461.9
    ② 473.8
    ③ 473.9 + 487.1
    ④ 487.1 + 461.9

80. The patient was assaulted and suffered a periorbital hematoma, nasal bone fracture, and chipped tooth.
    ① 921.2 + 802.0 + 873.63 + E960.0
    ② 921.2 + 802.0 + 873.79 + E960.0
    ③ 921.3 + 802.0 + 873.63 + E960.0
    ④ 921.9 + 802.0 + 873.79 + E960.0

81. Select the correct code(s) for a hiatal hernia with obstruction.
    ① 552.3
    ② 552.9
    ③ 553.8
    ④ 750.6

82. Patient complains of insomnia.
    ① 307.42
    ② 307.49
    ③ 780.51
    ④ 780.52

83. Patient is evaluated for sudden total blindness of the right eye; left eye was not affected.
    ① 368.60
    ② 369.60
    ③ 369.63
    ④ 369.64

84. Select the correct code for cardiac asthma.
    ① 428.1
    ② 428.22
    ③ 493.20
    ④ 493.90

85. Adult male was diagnosed with whooping cough due to parapertussis.
    ① 033.1
    ② 033.9
    ③ 306.1
    ④ 786.2

86. Patient was suffering from near-syncope episodes and was diagnosed with an electrolyte imbalance.
    ① 276.0
    ② 276.4
    ③ 276.50
    ④ 276.9

87. Patient is HIV positive and now has evidence of Kaposi lesions on the skin.
    ① 042
    ② 042 + 176.0
    ③ 757.33
    ④ 176.0 + V08

88. A female in her third trimester of pregnancy has obvious dependent edema.
    ① 643.80
    ② 646.10
    ③ 646.13
    ④ 646.20

89. The patient has been diagnosed with multiple sclerosis.
    ① 337.9
    ② 340
    ③ 341.8
    ④ 341.9

90. Select the correct code for a pathologic fracture of the distal radius.
    ① 733.10
    ② 733.12
    ③ 733.19
    ④ 813.42

91. The patient was seen today for arthritis related to a salmonella infection.
    ① 003.0
    ② 003.20
    ③ 003.23
    ④ 003.8

92. Female diagnosed with Darling's endocarditis.
    ① 115.00
    ② 115.03
    ③ 115.04
    ④ 115.09

93. The patient worked with talc for many years and is now diagnosed with pneumoconiosis.
    ① 500
    ② 502
    ③ 503
    ④ 505

94. A 17-year-old male has second degree burns of both ankles and feet caused by fireworks.
    ① 945.03 + E923.0
    ② 945.23 + E923.0
    ③ 945.29 + E923.0
    ④ 946.2 + E923.0

95. The patient will take an early retirement due to complications of post-polio syndrome.

   ① 045.12

   ② 045.90

   ③ 046.1

   ④ 138

96. An elderly woman is seen for multiple neuropathies following shingles.

   ① 053.10

   ② 053.13

   ③ 353.8

   ④ 356.4

97. The patient fell from his horse and was diagnosed with a C2 fracture and posterior cord syndrome.

   ① 806.00 + E828.2

   ② 806.04 + E828.2

   ③ 806.09 + E827.2

   ④ 805.19 + E827.2

98. A 78-year-old became comatose when given the insulin ordered for the patient in the next bed.

   ① 250.30

   ② 962.3

   ③ 995.23

   ④ 995.4

99. The patient was diagnosed with septicemia secondary to anthrax.

   ① 022.0

   ② 022.3

   ③ 022.8

   ④ 038.9

100. The patient received a laceration of the carotid artery while harvesting hay.

   ① 900.00 + E920.8

   ② 900.00 + E919.0

   ③ 900.01 + E919.8

   ④ 998.2 + E920.8

Name _____

Answers to Exam Questions: ICD-9-CM

1. ① ② ③ ④
2. ① ② ③ ④
3. ① ② ③ ④
4. ① ② ③ ④
5. ① ② ③ ④
6. ① ② ③ ④
7. ① ② ③ ④
8. ① ② ③ ④
9. ① ② ③ ④
10. ① ② ③ ④
11. ① ② ③ ④
12. ① ② ③ ④
13. ① ② ③ ④
14. ① ② ③ ④
15. ① ② ③ ④
16. ① ② ③ ④
17. ① ② ③ ④
18. ① ② ③ ④
19. ① ② ③ ④
20. ① ② ③ ④
21. ① ② ③ ④
22. ① ② ③ ④
23. ① ② ③ ④
24. ① ② ③ ④
25. ① ② ③ ④
26. ① ② ③ ④
27. ① ② ③ ④
28. ① ② ③ ④
29. ① ② ③ ④
30. ① ② ③ ④
31. ① ② ③ ④
32. ① ② ③ ④
33. ① ② ③ ④
34. ① ② ③ ④
35. ① ② ③ ④
36. ① ② ③ ④
37. ① ② ③ ④
38. ① ② ③ ④
39. ① ② ③ ④
40. ① ② ③ ④
41. ① ② ③ ④
42. ① ② ③ ④
43. ① ② ③ ④
44. ① ② ③ ④
45. ① ② ③ ④
46. ① ② ③ ④
47. ① ② ③ ④
48. ① ② ③ ④
49. ① ② ③ ④
50. ① ② ③ ④
51. ① ② ③ ④
52. ① ② ③ ④
53. ① ② ③ ④
54. ① ② ③ ④
55. ① ② ③ ④
56. ① ② ③ ④
57. ① ② ③ ④
58. ① ② ③ ④
59. ① ② ③ ④
60. ① ② ③ ④
61. ① ② ③ ④
62. ① ② ③ ④
63. ① ② ③ ④
64. ① ② ③ ④
65. ① ② ③ ④
66. ① ② ③ ④
67. ① ② ③ ④
68. ① ② ③ ④
69. ① ② ③ ④
70. ① ② ③ ④
71. ① ② ③ ④
72. ① ② ③ ④
73. ① ② ③ ④
74. ① ② ③ ④
75. ① ② ③ ④
76. ① ② ③ ④
77. ① ② ③ ④
78. ① ② ③ ④
79. ① ② ③ ④
80. ① ② ③ ④
81. ① ② ③ ④
82. ① ② ③ ④
83. ① ② ③ ④
84. ① ② ③ ④
85. ① ② ③ ④
86. ① ② ③ ④
87. ① ② ③ ④
88. ① ② ③ ④
89. ① ② ③ ④
90. ① ② ③ ④
91. ① ② ③ ④
92. ① ② ③ ④
93. ① ② ③ ④
94. ① ② ③ ④
95. ① ② ③ ④
96. ① ② ③ ④
97. ① ② ③ ④
98. ① ② ③ ④
99. ① ② ③ ④
100. ① ② ③ ④

Appendix—Selected Answers

Worksheet Answers

Evaluation and Management - I
2012 CPT Codes 99201–99239
1. 99217
3. 99204-25 or 99205-25
5. 99213
7. 99221
9. 99212
11. 99233
13. 99235

Evaluation and Management - II
2012 CPT Codes 99241–99340
1. 99243
3. 99253-57 or 99254-57
5. 99318
7. 99255
9. 99325
11. 99245
13. 99253
15. 99339

Evaluation and Management - III
2012 CPT Codes 99341–99499
1. 99347
3. 99477
5. 99366
7. 99461
9. 99386
11. 99360 q=2
13. 99393
15. 99344

Anesthesia Services
2012 CPT Codes 00100–01999
1. 01935
3. 01960
5. 01486-P3
7. 00214 and 99100
9. 00160
11. 00670
13. 01925
15. 01622

Integumentary System
2012 CPT Codes 10021–19499
1. 15776
3. 11981
5. 13160
7. 11750-TA
9. 11100
11. 17110
13. 19000-RT
15. 12002
17. 11450-RT
19. 11622
21. 16030
23. 11012
25. 15835-RT

Musculoskeletal System - I
2012 CPT Codes 20000–23929
1. 20206-RT
3. 20950-RT
5. 21116-LT
7. 23331-RT
9. 21049
11. 20694
13. 23800-RT
15. 23472-RT
17. 22222 and 22226 q=1
19. 23044-LT
21. 20973-TA
23. 20101-RT
25. 22830

Musculoskeletal System - II
2012 CPT Codes 23930–27299
1. 26045-LT
3. 26665-FA
5. 24100-RT
7. 25240-LT
9. 24685-LT
11. 25400-LT
13. 26560-RT
15. 25931-F1
17. 24566-LT
19. 26236-F3
21. 25449-LT
23. 26554-LT
25. 24342-LT

Musculoskeletal System - III
2012 CPT Codes 27301–29999
1. 29825-RT
3. 27331-LT
5. 29874-LT
7. 27524-LT
9. 28264-RT
11. 27603-LT
13. 27507-LT
15. 27695-RT
17. 27685-LT
19. 27422-RT
21. 27882-LT
23. 28530-LT
25. 28755-T5

Respiratory System
2012 CPT Codes 30000–32999
1. 30130-LT
3. 31255
5. 31641
7. 31400
9. 32310
11. 31825
13. 31615
15. 31237
17. 30300
19. 31368
21. 30110
23. 31291
25. 32420-LT

Cardiovascular System
2012 CPT Codes 33010–37799
1. 37718-LT
3. 33534 and 33517
5. 33222
7. 33736
9. 36000-LT
11. 33915
13. 33945
15. 36600
17. 35636
19. 35112
21. 33011
23. 33476
25. 33681

Hemic/Lymph/Medias/Diaphragm
2012 CPT Codes 38100–39599
1. 38505
3. 39540
5. 38300-LT
7. 38525-RT
9. 38308
11. 38101
13. 38564
15. 38221
17. 39545
19. 38240
21. 39220
23. 38555-LT
25. 38571

Digestive System
2012 CPT Codes 40490–49999
1. 42700
3. 43846
5. 44147
7. 49500
9. 46221
11. 44391
13. 49220 and 44015
15. 40844
17. 45910
19. 43425
21. 47120

161

23. 47802
25. 42950

Urinary System
2012 CPT Codes 50010–53899
1. 53601 or 53621
3. 50500
5. 52234
7. 50815
9. 51784
11. 52283
13. 50045
15. 53250
17. 50610
19. 52318
21. 51725
23. 50393
25. 52648

Male Genital System
2012 CPT Codes 54000–55899
1. 54150
3. 55700
5. 55840
7. 55870
9. 55250
11. 55110
13. 55860
15. 54535
17. 55650
19. 54560-50
21. 54865
23. 54420
25. 55400

Intersex/FemGenital/Maternity
2012 CPT Codes 55920–59899
1. 58545
3. 58974
5. 57460
7. 59821
9. 59015
11. 58340
13. 59409 and 59412
15. 57545
17. 57720
19. 58240
21. 59515
23. 57288
25. 58559

Endocrine and Nervous Systems
2012 CPT Codes 60000–64999
1. 60254
3. 64760
5. 64893-LT
7. 63081
9. 61791
11. 64435
13. 61606
15. 61526
17. 61250-50
19. 63040

21. 60605
23. 64898-LT and 64902–51-LT
25. 62141

Eye and Ocular Adnexa
2012 CPT Codes 65091–68899
1. 68811-LT
3. 67413-LT
5. 65150-RT
7. 65260-LT
9. 66625-LT
11. 67904-RT
13. 67112-LT
15. 65286-RT
17. 68530-RT
19. 66820-LT
21. 66984-LT
23. 68761-RT q=1
25. 67318-LT

Auditory System
2012 CPT Codes 69000–69990
1. 69710-LT
3. 69740 and 69990
5. 69145-RT
7. 69440-LT
9. 69820-LT
11. 69400-LT
13. 69745-LT
15. 69110-RT
17. 69540-LT
19. 69000-LT
21. 69910-LT
23. 69642-RT
25. 69220-RT

Radiology – I
2012 CPT Codes 70010–73725
1. 73580-26-LT
3. 73564-RT
5. 70492
7. 70030-LT
9. 71010
11. 70555
13. 72141
15. 72040-26
17. 71110
19. 73510-LT
21. 73010-LT
23. 71550
25. 72240-26

Radiology – II
2012 CPT Codes 74000–76499
1. 74241
3. 74230
5. 76120-26
7. 74455-26
9. 75961-26
11. 74270
13. 75680-26
15. 75887-26
17. 75791-26

19. 75605-26
21. 75801-26-RT
23. 74320-26
25. 75563-26

Radiology – III
2012 CPT Codes 76506–79999
1. 76805 and 76810 q=1
3. 77285-RT
5. 78195
7. 77408
9. 76872
11. 78272
13. 76516
15. 78135
17. 77326
19. 79440
21. 78805
23. 76828
25. 78205

Pathology and Laboratory – I
2012 CPT Codes 80047–83887
1. 80426
3. 82270
5. 82131 q=3
7. 82055
9. 82190
11. 81000
13. 82575
15. 83045
17. 80101
19. 81025
21. 80074
23. 80412
25. 80439

Pathology and Laboratory – II
2012 CPT Codes 83890–86849
1. 84181
3. 84030
5. 84446
7. 83896 q=1
9. 85240
11. 86140
13. 85525
15. 84525
17. 84703
19. 84403
21. 84133
23. 84620
25. 86225

Pathology and Laboratory – III
2012 CPT Codes 86850–89356
1. 86965
3. 88349
5. 88045
7. 88182
9. 87804
11. 88304
13. 89320
15. 87184 q=10

17. 88267
19. 88125
21. 86927 q=2
23. 88362
25. 88331 and 88332 q=1

Medicine – I
2012 CPT Codes 90281–92700
1. 92286
3. 90385
5. 92512
7. 91122
9. 92081-RT
11. 90747 and 90471
13. 90959
15. 90846
17. 92235
19. 92567
21. 92552
23. 90870
25. 90827

Medicine – II
2012 CPT Codes 92950–96020
1. 92977
3. 93660-26
5. 95868
7. 93888
9. 95827
11. 95004 q=10, and 95010 q=3
13. 93225
15. 95970
17. 93600
19. 93965
21. 94760
23. 93351
25. 95933

Medicine – III
2012 CPT Codes 96040–0290T
1. 99507
3. 97033 q=2
5. 98925
7. 98968
9. 3288F
11. 96902
13. 96154 q=2
15. 99502
17. 97002
19. 99511
21. 96422
23. 96401
25. 99601

HCPCS Level II Codes
2012 HCPCS
1. V5060
3. J0558
5. M0300
7. L3360-RT
9. J0780
11. A4358
13. Q0091
15. A0130
17. E0105
19. J9280
21. L6707
23. A4210
25. E0619

Modifiers
2012 CPT and HCPCS
1. 24
3. 32
5. 57
7. AH
9. QD
11. AR

Infectious/Parasitic Diseases – I
2012 ICD-9-CM (001–139)
1. 003, A02
3. 138, B91
5. 054, B00
7. 101, A69
9. 099, A56

Infectious/Parasitic Diseases – II
2012 ICD-9-CM (001–139)
1. 077.0, B30.1
3. 100.89, A77.3
5. 110.9, B35.9
7. 090.5, A50.57
9. 061, A90
11. 004.0, A03.0
13. 051.1, B08.03
15. 002.9, A01.4
17. 062.4, A83.4
19. 038.3, A41.4
21. 030.2, A30.9
23. 065.8, A98.4
25. 084.4, B53.1

Neoplasms – I
2012 ICD-9-CM (140–239)
1. 141, C02
3. 232, D04
5. 157, C25
7. 233, D05
9. 162, C34

Neoplasms – II
2012 ICD-9-CM (140–239)
1. 151.0, C16.0
3. 140.9, C00.2
5. 198.5, C79.51
7. 191.9, C71.9
9. 239.5, D49.5
11. 197.6, C78.6
13. 223.1, D30.11
15. 158.8, C48.1
17. 228.1, D18.1
19. 231.1, D02.1
21. 202.84, C85.94
23. 165.8, C39.9
25. 146.2, C09.1

Endo/Nutri/Metabol/Immunity – I
2012 ICD-9-CM (240–279)
1. 272, E78
3. 242, E05
5. 259, E34
7. 265, E51
9. 246, E07

Endo/Nutri/Metabol/Immunity – II
2012 ICD-9-CM (240–279)
1. 250.50, E11.359
3. 261, E41
5. 270.7, E72.51
7. 250.31, E10.11
9. 242.01, E05.01
11. 261, E43
13. 275.49, E20.1
15. 279.13, D81.4
17. 271.3, E73.9
19. 255.0, E24.9
21. 276.3, E87.3
23. 241.9, E04.9
25. 268.0, E55.0

Blood/Blood-Forming – I
2012 ICD-9-CM (280–289)
1. 286, D67
3. 285, D64
5. 281, D51
7. 288, D72
9. 289, D75

Blood/Blood Forming – II
2012 ICD-9-CM (280–289)
1. 286.5, D68.31
3. 287.41, D69.59
5. 285.9, D64.9
7. 282.61, D57.1
9. 283.0, D59.1
11. 289.9, D75.9
13. 269.0, E56.1
15. 286.0, D66
17. 289.59, D73.89
19. 288.3, D72.1
21. 282.49, D56.8
23. 288.51, D72.810
25. 281.2, D52.0

Mental Disorders – I
2012 ICD-9-CM (290–319)
1. 300, F48
3. 297, F22
5. 307, F50
7. 312, F63
9. 291, F04

Mental Disorders – II
2012 ICD-9-CM (290–319)
1. 300.7, F45.20
3. 300.21, F40.01
5. 301.51, F68.10
7. 300.11, F45.8
9. 306.0, F45.41

11. 314.01, F90.9
13. 296.02, F30.12
15. 304.31, F12.288
17. 302.51, F64.1
19. 295.34, F20.0
21. 302.81, F65.0
23. 302.76, F52.6
25. 299.10, F84.3

Nervous System/Sense Organs – I
2012 ICD-9-CM (320–389)
1. 320, G00
3. 366, H25
5. 368, H53
7. 333, G25
9. 371, H18

Nervous System/Sense Organs – II 2012 ICD-9-CM (320–389)
1. 362.21, H35.173
3. 334.0, G11.1
5. 327.21, G47.31
7. 385.30, H71.22
9. 371.41, H18.411
11. 357.0, G61.0
13. 357.7 or 349.82, G92 or G62.2
15. 355.6, G57.62
17. 331.81, G93.7
19. 331.4, G91.1
21. 362.54, H35.342
23. 363.21, H30.20
25. 366.51, H26.412

Circulatory System – I
2012 ICD-9-CM (390–459)
1. 415, I26
3. 425, I42
5. 457, I89
7. 448, I78
9. 440, I70

Circulatory System – II
2012 ICD-9-CM (390–459)
1. 427.81, I49.5
3. 446.1, M30.0
5. 402.91, I11.0
7. 426.53, I45.2
9. 391.1, I01.1
11. 459.2, I87.1
13. 425.2, I42.8
15. 427.32, I48.1
17. 435.2, G45.8
19. 454.1, I87.2
21. 457.8, I89.8
23. 426.7, I45.6
25. 413.1, I20.1

Respiratory System – I
2012 ICD-9-CM (460–519)
1. 477, J30
3. 507, J69
5. 464, J04
7. 519, J98
9. 471, J33

Respiratory System – II
2012 ICD-9-CM (460–519)
1. 488.11, J09.119
3. 516.32, J84.1
5. 518.89, J98.09
7. 495.3, J67.3
9. 512.1, J95.81
11. 477.9, J30.9
13. 482.82, J15.5
15. 500, J60
17. 462, J02.9
19. 463, J03.90
21. 482.84, A48.1
23. 460, J00
25. 493.90, J45.909

Digestive System – I
2012 ICD-9-CM (520–579)
1. 571, K70
3. 575, K81
5. 579, K90
7. 527, K11
9. 577, K85

Digestive System – II
2012 ICD-9-CM (520–579)
1. 578.0, K92.0
3. 572.1, K75.1
5. 529.3, K14.3
7. 564.4, K91.1
9. 531.00, K25.0
11. 550.01, K40.41
13. 527.2, K11.20
15. 527.5, K11.5
17. 528.4, K09.1
19. 575.6, K82.4
21. 567.22, K65.1
23. 535.30, K29.20
25. 542, K36

Genitourinary System – I
2012 ICD-9-CM (580–629)
1. 585, N18
3. 601, N41
5. 626, N92
7. 617, N80
9. 606, N46

Genitourinary System – II
2012 ICD-9-CM (580–629)
1. 599.0, N39.0
3. 611.1, N62
5. 606.8, N46.124
7. 614.3, N73.0
9. 617.4, N80.4
11. 616.2, N75.0
13. 622.0, N86
15. 596.51, N32.81
17. 593.0, N28.89
19. 617.1, N80.1
21. 607.1, N48.1
23. 628.0, N97.0
25. 620.1, N83.1

Preg/Childbirth/Puerperium – I
2012 ICD-9-CM (630–679)
1. 671, O22
3. 633, O00
5. 653, O33
7. 642, O13
9. 651, O30

Preg/Childbirth/Puerperium – II
2012 ICD-9-CM (630–679)
1. 671.33, O22.30
3. 634.51, O03.31
5. 651.81, O30.809
7. 674.12, O90.0
9. 688.10, O74.2
11. 666.02, O72.0
13. 646.13, O12.00
15. 665.72, O71.7
17. 646.23, O26.839
19. 640.00, O20.0
21. 659.33, O75.3
23. 652.21, O32.1xx0
25. 635.30, O04.82

Skin and Subcutaneous Tissue – I
2012 ICD-9-CM (680–709)
1. 707, L89
3. 694, L10
5. 703, L60
7. 704, L63
9. 709, L80

Skin and Subcutaneous Tissue – II 2012 ICD-9-CM (680–709)
1. 693.8, L27.8
3. 698.3, L28.0
5. 694.0, L13.0
7. 707.20, L89.019
9. 680.0, L02.02
11. 692.82, L56.4
13. 695.4, L93.0
15. 691.0, L22
17. 705.81, L30.1
19. 696.3, L42
21. 684, L01.1
23. 692.83, L23.0
25. 705.1, L74.2

Musculo/Connective Tissue – I
2012 ICD-9-CM (710–739)
1. 714, M05
3. 717, M23
5. 738, M95
7. 725, M35
9. 721, M48

Musculo/Connective Tissue – II
2012 ICD-9-CM (710–739)
1. 727.06, M65.872
3. 717.7, M22.42
5. 728.88, M62.82
7. 711.00, M00.00
9. 717.41, M23.262

11. 737.21, M96.4
13. 710.20, M35.03
15. 722.93, M51.86
17. 723.5, M43.6
19. 736.79, M21.372
21. 736.42, M21.169
23. 724.2, M54.5
25. 728.83, M62.112

Congenital Anomalies – I
2012 ICD-9-CM (740–759)
1. 743, Q11
3. 754, Q67
5. 744, Q16
7. 745, Q21
9. 755, Q65

Congenital Anomalies – II
2012 ICD-9-CM (740–759)
1. 755.39, Q72.892
3. 755.57, Q74.0
5. 759.0, Q89.09
7. 743.20, Q15.0
9. 747.10, Q25.1
11. 752.51, Q53.9
13. 744.03, Q16.4
15. 758.0, Q90.9
17. 746.86, Q24.6
19. 748.4, Q33.0
21. 759.82, Q87.40
23. 752.7, Q56.3
25. 748.1, Q30.2

Conditions of Perinatal Period – I 2012 ICD-9-CM (760–779)
1. 760, O25
3. 766, O33
5. 764, P05
7. 767, P13
9. 775, P70

Conditions of Perinatal Period – II 2012 ICD-9-CM (760–779)
1. 762.6, O69.5xx0
3. 771.2, P37.2
5. 770.6, P22.1
7. 760.70, P04.49
9. 766.22, P08.22
11. 769, P22.0
13. 760.71, Q86.0
15. 773.1, P55.1

17. 779.9, P95
19. 775.6, P70.4
21. 768.6, P84
23. 774.4, P59.29
25. 776.1, P61.0

Symptoms/Ill-Defined Cond – I
2012 ICD-9-CM (780–799)
1. 799, R09
3. 783, R63
5. 785, R57
7. 786, R06
9. 787, R19

Symptoms/Ill-Defined Cond – II
2012 ICD-9-CM (780–799)
1. 792.1, R19.5
3. 784.51, R47.1
5. 787.3, R14.0
7. 786.50, R07.9
9. 791.6, R82.4
11. 782.62, R23.2
13. 783.1, R63.5
15. 795.51, R76.1
17. 780.4, R42
19. 788.20, R33.9
21. 784.99, R19.6
23. 780.79, R53.83
25. 782.3, R60.9

Injury and Poisoning – I
2012 ICD-9-CM (800–999)
1. 960, T36
3. 842, S63
5. 801, S02
7. 996, T82
9. 832, S53

Injury and Poisoning – II
2012 ICD-9-CM (800–999)
1. 999.1, T80.0xxS
3. 873.0, S01.01xD
5. 831.04, S43.101A
7. 995.81, T74.11xD
9. 988.1, T62.0x1A
11. 942.34, T21.33xA
13. 919.5, S80.869A
15. 825.35, S92.302B
17. 996.54, T85.43xA
19. 813.41, S52.531A
21. 807.2, S22.20xG

23. 845.00, S93.409A
25. 931, T16.2xxA

"V" Codes – I
2012 ICD-9-CM (V01–V91)
1. V85, Z68
3. V25, Z30
5. V34, Z38
7. V06, Z23
9. V01, Z20

"V" Codes – II
2012 ICD-9-CM (V01–V91)
1. V25.02, Z30.09
3. V27.3, Z37.3
5. V61.21, Z62.819
7. V59.5, Z52.5
9. V44.50, Z43.5
11. V64.07, Z28.1
13. V10.61, Z85.6
15. V72.5, Z00.00
17. V53.4, Z46.4
19. V72.31, Z01.419
21. V01.0, Z20.09
23. V20.31, Z00.110
25. V43.22, Z95.812

"E" Codes – I
2012 ICD-9-CM (E800–E999)
1. E801, V81
3. E847, V98
5. E850, T39
7. E906, W56
9. E917, W52

"E" Codes – II
2012 ICD-9-CM (E800–E999)
1. E905.6, T63.631A
3. E965.0, X93.xxxA
5. E826.1, V17.0xxA
7. E928.1, H83.3x9A
9. E883.0, W16.522A
11. E813.5, V80.42xA
13. E862.1, T52.0x1A
15. E997.2, Y36.7x0S
17. E946.5, Y84.8
19. E904.2, X58.xxxA
21. E832.9, T75.1xxA
23. E919.4, W31.2xxA
25. E901.1, W93.01xA

Instructions for Submitting an Exam to Delmar for CEU Approval

The American Academy of Professional Coders (AAPC) is granting approval for CEU credits to qualified candidates for the successful completion of the 30-question exam associated with 2012 Coding Workbook for the Physician's Office, ISBN, 978-1-111-64100-9 by Alice Covell. The AAPC will grant prior approval for a total of three (3) CEU credits for completion of this exam with a passing grade of 70% or better. To apply for CEU credit on this title, you will need to print out the exam posted to the Online Companion site for the 2012 workbook and return the completed exam to Delmar Cengage Learning for grading. For further instructions, access the Online Companion site by going to www.cengagebrain.com. In the search field in the upper right corner of the screen, type "Covell," then scroll down and select the link for the 2012 edition.

Please note: Awarding of a CEU certificate from Delmar Cengage Learning does not constitute full CEU approval. You will be responsible for submitting the awarded certificate to the AAPC the next time your credential is up for renewal in order to officially obtain the CEU credit(s).

This program has the prior approval of the American Academy of Professional Coders (AAPC) for 3 continuing education hours. Grant of prior approval in no way constitutes endorsement by the AAPC of the program content or program sponsor.
For more information on obtaining CEUs, please go to www.aapc.com